He Speaks

An extraordinary life with an extraordinary God.

REBECCA SCHWARTZKOPF

authorHOUSE®

AuthorHouse™
1663 Liberty Drive
Bloomington, IN 47403
www.authorhouse.com
Phone: 833-262-8899

Published by AuthorHouse 10/22/2020

ISBN: 978-1-7283-6994-5 (sc)
ISBN: 978-1-7283-6993-8 (e)

Print information available on the last page.

SPECIAL ACKNOWLEDGEMENTS

Thank you to Editors; Ann Wolf, Amelia Schwartzkopf, Catherine Hicks and Shona Deckert. Your help with editing this book was invaluable to me. How blessed am I to have such wonderful and talented friends (and daughter) like you.

DEDICATION

I would like to dedicate this book to my family. My husband Eric and our kids, Caleb, Kathryn and Amelia. Without your love, support, help and encouragement, I never would have finished this project. It literally takes a family.

PART I

LISTENING BEFORE I KNEW I WAS HEARING

Have you ever heard God speak? If you would have asked me this 4 years ago, I would have answered no. And while that might not be the case, that was my perception at the time. The fact is, I have heard Him speak, and a whole lot more than I ever even realized. God is speaking all the time; I just didn't know how to perceive it, to put weight to it, or even acknowledge it. It wasn't until recently that I realized He had been speaking clearly to me from my beginnings and continues to do so.

My heart in writing this book is to be a catalyst to get you, dear reader, to look back over your own life to see what you might have thought was coincidence, happenstance or karma as really being God. So that you, like me, will see just how invested He is in you: to feel His love for you and to know He sees you. This is my journey of hearing God and the lessons I've learned: the hard times and my hardness of heart and how God changed, delivered and softened me. This is not my story but His story—His speaking into an ordinary life.

In 2019, a few friends and I decided to attend a prophetic conference at Bethel Church in Redding, CA. Prior to the conference, I really didn't know much about prophecy, except what I was learning at my own church in Walla Walla, Washington, where I've lived for several years with my husband and kids.

In the Protestant Churches I attended, we didn't talk

much about how God talks to us personally through His Holy Spirit. I wasn't aware of the power that we, as followers of Jesus Christ, have in Him. Not only the power to hear His voice but to show the world that He exists, that He is amazing, and that He is "able to do immeasurably more than all we can ask or imagine" (Ephesians 3:21, NIV).

When I realized what I had been missing, I decided to attend the multi-day conference. While my friends and I were in a workshop, a stranger turned around and looked at me with this crazy fish stare and said, "Write a book, you need to write a book. It doesn't have to be long, but you need to write it." I looked over my shoulder to see if someone was sitting behind me who she might be talking to. Nope, she was talking to me.

Thinking about it afterwards, I remembered I had kicked around the idea of writing a book about 15 years ago. But at that time thought, "What would I say? What would it be about? Would it be a devotional or perhaps a book on parenting? Or, would the focus be what I have learned at the feet of Jesus?" I also pondered, "Would anybody else want to read it, or was it just for me and not for another's eyes?"

After much prayer and many false starts, I felt the Lord asking me to look back, literally, through the pages of my life to find Him. He said to me, "You have to go back to go forward." I believe that taking this look back will be the catalyst to my moving past myself, my pride, my insecurities and frankly my own unbelief. God has always been there, has always loved me and has always talked to me. I have heard Him, but I've never really put it together that He was actually talking to me.

The point is, God does speak. It might be through the Word—those times when you read something in the Bible, and it goes straight to your heart and fits exactly what you are going through. On the other hand, it may be that you hear an audible voice. Once when I was driving home and cresting the hill on a four-lane highway, I heard a very stern and audible, "GET OVER!" I immediately got over, and as I neared the top of the hill a car was coming the wrong way in the passing lane. Had I not switched lanes we would have had a head-on collision with both of us going about 55 mph.

Not only can God speak in these ways, but I have also heard Him through situations or themes that He repeats over and over until I finally "get" it. When I finally realized that He truly wants to talk to me I started watching for Him.

One night after the prophetic conference, I woke up feeling like He was saying, "I want you to do this, to write this." Initially I hesitated. I had always thought that speaking was my gift. I asked Him why He hadn't let me speak and He replied, "It would have destroyed you." He was right. You see, in my insecurity, I experienced a heightened desire to be seen. I would have made it about me and stolen His glory like I have many times before. But right now, in writing this book, I am out of my depth— right where He wants me. The glory is His alone.

CONFIRMATIONS

The thought of writing this book was daunting, but God, in His sweetness, has lifted me up at every turn. Amidst the doubt, the uncertainty and my own hesitancy during this process, the Lord has been kind to encourage me at different points along the way.

When I was first exhorted to write this book, I thought, "How can this even be possible? This is so far beyond me." That's when I heard it—a small voice, just behind me and to my left, so quiet I almost missed it. The voice said, "I will help you." It was the same voice that I'd heard a few years ago. We were selling our home and had already purchased a new one. I was fearful of having two mortgages. I said, "Lord, I am so freaked out that I don't even know what to pray, so I'm just going to pray in my prayer language." As I was looking out the window and praying, I heard very softly, almost behind me, "Trust me." I responded: "Ok." We moved and put the house on the market, and it sold in the first week. Many other homes were on the market at the time and just as nice or nicer than ours, but they weren't selling. So, when I heard that same voice, in the same place, promising me His help, I was willing to try.

I used to get mad at God, and say, "You say in Your Word, specifically in Isaiah 30:21, 'whether you turn right or left, you will hear a voice behind you saying, This is the way, walk in it.'" And I would say, "I am not hearing You!" When thinking about those last two exchanges, however, I realized His voice had come from behind me!

Another time I was feeling as if maybe I had just misunderstood God and I really wasn't supposed to write this. But God was ready. My husband has a friend named Steve and they were talking one day. Steve asked my husband if I was writing a book. Eric said, "Did I tell you she was?" Steve replied, "No, but when I was praying for her, I saw her bent over a desk writing, writing, writing. I thought maybe she is writing a book." He said, "Yes! She is writing a book." Craziness!

Countless times I've been in a conference or listening to a speaker talking about the hard things God often asks us to do. To my surprise, they always seem to use "writing a book" as an example. In those moments I could just shout: "Are you kidding me?!" I am so amazed by God's goodness and His humor.

Several of the confirmations and encouragements I have received I have experienced within my own family. My daughter Kathryn (Kat) had many words for me while writing this book. On one of these occasions she saw a big ship traveling through ice, barely moving. Once it got moving through the ice, however, there was a current under it that was pulling it forward. Most recently, I was with my son Caleb in Kenya. We had been on a safari and our Maasai guide, Alison, asked me what I did back home. I sheepishly said I was writing a book. He asked what it was about, and I said it was about my life with Jesus. He responded, "That is a book I would like to read." As we were driving away, I felt panic: "Dear God, I don't know if I can do this or if I can finish it!" I looked out the window and at that moment we were passing a church. The name of the church, written in big bold letters was, "GOD IS ABLE." He never fails to answer my fears when I call out to Him and even when I don't.

Before I go on any further I think it's important to include a word of caution. Not all messages and impressions you receive are from God. The Bible says "your enemy the devil prowls around like a roaring lion looking for someone to devour" (1 Peter 5:8 NIV). Satan would like nothing more than to confuse you. Because we know God is love and He is holy, we know He does not lie. That means He will not act contrary to what He has revealed in His written word. If you feel you have heard God speak to you in a manner that is inconsistent with what He says in the Bible, always defer to what the scriptures say and seek Godly counsel.

2 Timothy 3: 16-17 is very clear about the authority of Scripture:

> All Scripture is inspired by God and is useful to teach us what is true and to make us realize what is wrong in our lives. It corrects us when we are wrong and teaches us to do what is right. God uses it to prepare and equip his people to do every good work (NLT).

BEGINNINGS

I was born into a troubled home. My mom was 21 when she had me. I was the last of her three children. For the most part, my dad was unmotivated, uninterested and uninvolved. For a short time, he had a good job selling insurance. He was a good salesman but for some reason he hated working for anyone, so the good job and good times didn't last long. He quit his job, bought a bar and thus started his downward spiral of drinking, drugs and women.

My mom knew she had to get out and away from my dad, so she started beauty school to support us. It took her longer than most because she had to wait until I was in school. She took summers off because she didn't want to take us to the sitter, nor could we afford one. I have an incredible mom, born with an indomitable spirit. She knew what she needed to do and set about doing it. Once she was graduated, we were out of there.

I put my faith and trust in Jesus when I was young, probably at about six years old. I can remember sitting in the pew with my mom drawing on the offering envelope and not paying any attention. When the pastor gave the altar call, I just remember being in a state of panic. "I've got to go!" My mom grabbed my arm and said, "Where are you going?" I kept trying to pull away, just repeating, "Mom! I've got to go!!" The sense of urgency was so strong that I could not get away fast enough. I remember saying, "If I don't go, I could die and not go to heaven."

Now, some might take exception to that kind of conversion, but in all honesty, the day I put my faith and trust in Jesus was the best day ever, however, it wasn't very long after that when our world fell apart. First, my grandfather died after a long illness, then my parents divorced, and we started a progression of moving every two years -- new apartment, new school.

In the turmoil of constant change, I always knew that the Lord was with me. I always had a sense of joy. Money was always an issue and yet God always provided. We never felt the pinch of a lack of money. Sometimes people would put money in my hand to give to my mom. The necessities were always there, needs were always met.

Not long ago I was looking at an old photo album, in which were pictures of a Christmas long ago and I was sitting in the middle of a crazy assortment of gifts. You see, my mother did hair in a nursing home and that year our gifts consisted of crafts the residents had made. Looking at the picture I could see that I was nothing but happy. I never noticed anything out of the ordinary, until I looked back as an adult. God was always there, unseen.

I can remember a day when I was in the fifth—sixth grade and I had missed the bus. My mom was already at work, and I was late. I knew I was going to have to walk, so I set off. It was taking a lot longer than I was anticipating and

I was going to be late, so I decided to take a shortcut using the railroad tracks. There was only one problem. Halfway between me and the school there was an abandoned rail/freight car and it scared me. As I started walking closer to it my apprehension grew and I stopped. I didn't know what to do. I was going to be late.

I stood there looking back at the road, looking forward at the rail car and looking back again, as I squared my shoulders to continue, I heard the voice of a woman from behind me and she was yelling at me. She was in her car, sitting on the tracks and she told me to get in the car right that instant. She was so irate that I walked back to her on the tracks without thinking. I sat in that car while she proceeded to berate me all the way to school about the dangers of walking on the railroad tracks and what could happen to young girls on them. But I didn't care -- I was safe and on time.

When I was 13, we moved from Toledo, Ohio, to Texas. My mom was going to get married and we were going to live happily ever after. I loved Texas. I loved the people, my school, our little house and neighborhood. I thought that, finally after all the crap with my dad, life was looking up.

Well, a month or so into it while we were all in school, my mother's fiancé up and left us. Within three days, bewildered and hurting, we packed everything up, left Texas and moved to Denver, Colorado. It was at this time that I learned to put my head down and just get through it.

It's interesting to me that, all the while we were looking at schools, I just knew I wasn't going to be going to school there. Have you ever had a sense that you "just knew" something, but you didn't know why? That's God. He knows our futures and sometimes He just lets us in on it to some degree.

After having a hard time getting back on her feet, my mom couldn't make it. It was decided that she needed to split up the family so that she could work on establishing a clientele as a hairdresser so she could support us. I moved to California to live with an uncle and my middle brother went back to Ohio to live with our grandmother while my oldest brother was old enough to stay and get a job to help out. After the school year and when most of the summer had ended, my brother and I both came back. While we were gone, my mom had met our stepdad. After a relatively short period, they were married.

It wasn't long after the marriage started that my stepdad's vicious temper was discovered. In less than a month, things took an extremely ugly turn. Yelling and screaming and fits of rage at least once a week became the norm. There was no telling what might provoke him, and it didn't take much.

In high school, I made one poor choice after another, drinking and partying, progressively getting worse as I went. Always with the desire to be "part of the group," to have friends, to be seen. I excelled in drinking and partying -- anything to not have to be me or think about my life or all the crap happening at home.

I put my head down and just tried to get through it. At 19, I got married to get out of the house away from a stepdad who was verbally abusive to my mother and me, and physically and verbally abusive to my brother. We were married in August and less than a year later, we were divorced. I was like a tornado destroying everything in my path.

CHRIST IN MY YOUTH

I developed an eating disorder at 20 years of age. After losing some weight, I found that I had a lot more guy friends and I liked the attention. Starving myself was not sustainable so I began binging and purging. I did that for the next 20 years. It was a cycle of being out of control, trying to control, self-loathing and hate. I remember thinking, "when I'm 40 I'm going to stop this." What an odd thought.

Odder still, it was the year I turned 40 that the Lord delivered me from it in a remarkable way. I divorced my husband a year after we married, and from the ages of 20 to 25 I plugged my ears and ran from God. He would nudge me every now and then. It felt like someone was tapping me on the shoulder and I would literally shrug it off. As I progressively got further and further away, He started to nudge harder and harder until I got the sense that if I didn't stop, I was going to self-destruct.

You could say that put the fear of God in me. I quit my traveling job, came home, greatly decreased my partying, got a job at a local hospital, met my husband and three years later we were married. I wish I could say, "and we all lived happily ever after," but being me and being the wife of a doctor, it was a very lonely road. Not that it's his fault, it's just the nature of the beast.

We moved to a small town in Nebraska and right away

we moved into the country. Isolated and alone, with only a one-month-old baby to keep me company, two things began to happen: I started drinking and getting serious about God. Wow, what a winning combination! I can remember going for long walks and being so upset by where we lived, and the long hours spent alone. My anger was building, and I spent most of my walks ranting at God.

You see, when Eric was interviewing for the job in North Platte, I was pregnant with our first child, Caleb. I had an abruption, where the placenta pulls away from the uterus prematurely, late in my 3rd trimester. I was on bed rest when Eric was scheduled to interview, so I stayed home while he went alone. He described it as such a great opportunity that I agreed to go sight unseen. Looking back, I would never have agreed had I been at the interview, but God had other plans. He wanted us to move, but He knew it would take a miracle to get me there.

When I arrived, the struggle really began. I remember reading Corrie ten Boom's book *The Hiding Place* during this time. On one occasion in the book, Betsy tells her sister Corrie she needs to be thankful for the lice in their barracks. Corrie refuses. Finally, after time, she relents and thanks God for the lice only to find out that it was the very presence of the pests that kept the guards away so they could study the Bible.

I was convicted by this account. Shortly after I came across it, I was on one of my frequent stroller-ranting walks.

With one fist waving in the air and one on the stroller, I thanked God for North Platte. I waited, but nothing happened. A few weeks later, however, I was reading my Bible and came across a verse in Acts 17:26-27:

> From one man he made all the nations,
> that they should inhabit the whole earth;
> and he marked out their appointed times in
> history and the boundaries of their lands.
> God did this so that they would seek him
> and perhaps reach out for him and find
> him, though he is not far from any one of
> us. (NIV)

Wow! When I read that verse my perspective immediately changed: "You put me here in this very place to find you, to seek after you. You see me!" That was when I came to know God as "El Roi" ("the God who sees me"). Something inside of me relaxed, and I was able to embrace and come to love North Platte. It was after this act of obedience that I really started being aware of the Holy Spirit speaking, acting and moving in my life, though I didn't realize it at the time. I just thoughtlessly accepted it.

I started praying for a church home. The process was slow: just when we thought we found a church, something would unsettle us in a teaching and we would continue the search.

On one particular day I turned on KJLT, our local

Christian radio station. The employees were having their yearly fundraiser and were interviewing a pastor from a local church. I remember them questioning him regarding people giving to the radio station and if he thought they were taking from the church. He said, "No, not at all. I consider the radio station a mission, and missions are the very heart of God." I immediately thought, "Please God, let them say the name of this pastor's church." Not surprisingly, the next words I heard were just that: North Platte Berean Church.

At Berean, we found our church home and family. I remember the first time I walked in. Satan's pushback team rode us the whole way there, out of the car, and up the steps. As we walked through the door, however, I was met with peace. I knew I was home. Those little demons were way outnumbered and had to flee.

We jumped into our church with both feet. I remember clearly when Eric came to me and said he thought we needed to start tithing on his entire paycheck. I thought, "What?" All I could think about was how we were going to pull it off. When the next paycheck arrived, Eric faithfully started to tithe. I was scared at first. Though I didn't pay the bills I knew how much money we had. That being said, not only were we able to pay our bills, but it was not long until we got a letter from the bank telling us that they had miscalculated our loan. We now had extra money every month. By being faithful, God supplied all our needs and He has been faithful to us to this day.

It was at Berean that I started reading my Bible more and attending Bible study. Still, there was something missing. I wanted more, I just didn't know how to explain it: what it was or how to go about getting it. On the flip side, I was still drinking, fully engaged in bulimia, depressed and lonely. It's amazing how, in the same moment, things can be going so well in one area and so awful in another.

STRIVINGS

Mentally I was in trouble, my mom saw the warning signs of depression from Texas. She finally called Eric and told him I needed help. (That's how much Eric and I saw each other). Between the hospital and the clinic, I was alone a lot. I started taking an antidepressant and life started looking up. Still, there was a deep desire in me for more, more in-depth study and a deeper understanding of the Word.

That's where I was mentally when I was first introduced to a Beth Moore Bible study. Through Beth Moore, I found what I was searching for: a deeper and more in-depth look at God's Word. Beth went into the meanings of the Hebrew and Greek words and the historical times we were studying. She made everything come alive. Unfortunately for me, I was in such a state of loneliness and isolation, experiencing such deep feelings of rejection, that I began to covet her ability to teach women. I wanted to be seen and viewed as important to the same extent that she was.

It all started when I did her study, "Breaking Free." After a couple of weeks listening to her help others, I thought, "I can do this." If I did Bible studies, people would see me, they would want to know me, I'd be important. So, I set about single-mindedly studying my Bible, not to have a relationship with Jesus but to achieve my new goal.

I gobbled it up like hogs to the slop. I use that metaphor because I wasn't thinking about my relationship with Jesus, just my determination to be seen and heard. It was about insecurity, emptiness and a lack of validation. I started memorizing. I even started cross-referencing the Bible until I discovered it had already been done.

At one point, I became aware that several of my friends were experiencing difficult circumstances. At that same time, I was in a group doing Beth Moore's study, "Believing God." I couldn't help but think my friends would be greatly encouraged by the study. As I worked through the materials, I could not get them off my mind. Finally, I asked the Lord, "Are you asking me to lead this Bible study?" I didn't really get an answer but, at the same time, these ladies were always on my heart. Sometimes God answers through burdens that don't go away. Finally, I said, "Lord, if you want me to do this, then these five ladies have to say yes." Bada bing, bada bang, bada boom—they were all in!

Unfortunately, with my mindset at the time, I thought if one Bible Study was good, more was better. I started multiple studies and I had as many as four a week. It was an uphill battle, and I felt like I was slogging through mud. People weren't committed, they didn't do their homework, or they didn't even show up. I'd come prepared and only have one or two ladies who, though they were there, were unprepared. Though I'd be miffed they didn't do their homework, I realized I could spoon feed them my knowledge. This made me even more indispensable. It's interesting to note that this battle was true for all the Bible studies I started except for the one I actually felt the Lord's leading to do.

This went on for years, but God was kind to me. His Word is always true and never returns void, even when mishandled by someone with ignoble intentions. Those who came to the study were fed. The Lord would allow me to start things like a Bible Study in a junior high school, opening doors that at first seemed closed. I would struggle to get it going, but once I handed it over to someone else it would begin to flourish. This happened time and time again. I was doing a right thing with the wrong motivation, but God in His infinite mercy still used me to bless others.

I am reminded of Paul when writing to the Philippians about those who preach the gospel:

> Some indeed preach Christ from envy and rivalry, but others from good will. The latter do so out of love, knowing that I am put here for the defense of the gospel. The former preach Christ out of selfish ambition, not sincerely, supposing that they can stir up trouble for me while I am in chains. But what does it matter? The important thing is that, in every way, whether from false motives or true, Christ is preached. And because of this I rejoice. (1:15-18, NIV)

I was fast becoming one who taught out of "envy and rivalry" and "selfish ambition." I was working hard on building MY ministry. The more I grew in knowledge, the more insecure I became. It was all about me. If someone would make a good point, I'd be bummed that it wasn't me. I felt so threatened. I walked around in great confidence in my ever-increasing knowledge and great insecurity when confronted with those who knew more. I was completely unaware of what was happening to me on the inside and that it was the Lord who was blocking so many of my endeavors.

I started dedicating more time to studying the Word. I'd dissect the Epistles for hours and hours. I was living such a dichotomy. I loved God so much and wanted to help others: I wanted them to truly know Him, love Him, experience Him and be free. While I was fighting for the freedom of others, my own chains of insecurity, emptiness and pain were increasingly tightening and choking me in a prison of my own making.

I started getting weary of always striving and nothing ever working out according to my plan. One day I snapped. I yelled at God: "God, I can't do this anymore. It's too much!" I remember clearly hearing in return, "Who asked you to?" His response scared me. "Am I doing this all on my own? Have I made it all up?" These questions were too much for me to process. The thought that I had done all this work for God when He never asked me to was deflating. In response I decided to quit all the things I was doing at church and all my Bible studies. I dropped everything, except the one Bible study I knew He had led me to do.

A funny thing happens when you serve so much in your church—to the point that you feel indispensable— and then decide to scale back to a more reasonable commitment. That is, they find someone else within the church to fill the void. The "irreplaceable" you gets replaced. Be careful how you view your role in relation to the body of Christ: allow others to step up and exercise their giftings. When we do it all, we rob others of a chance to experience community through service.

It took me awhile to get over the feeling of being out of the loop and disconnected. But by God's grace, I did not allow myself to get sucked back in. That's when I realized there actually were enough hours in a day!

When Jesus is talking to a crowd of ordinary people like you and me, He says something profound:

> Are you tired? Worn out? Burned out on religion? Come to Me. Get away with me and you'll recover your life. I'll show you how to take a real rest. Walk with Me and work with Me—watch how I do it. Learn the unforced rhythms of grace. I won't lay anything heavy or ill-fitting on you. Keep company with me and you'll

> learn to live freely and lightly. (Matthew 11:28-30, MSG)

I love that. Rest! Satan loves to keep us busy, especially doing good things, great things even, in and outside the church. The enemy wants us to be too busy to do what is best, like sitting at the feet of Jesus. We need to learn to discern between what is "good" and what is actually "best."

Even in this struggle, God was sure to remind me that He saw me and was aware of my every move. I remember one day while I was driving just thinking to myself, "God, I can't even see you anymore." Ahead of me was a viaduct that went over the railroad. As I looked ahead, I saw a flock of birds flying back and forth in between the guard rails. They were perched up high and would then swoop down over the road before flying up to the other side. I had never seen them do this before. As I approached, I thought for sure they would stop. Instead, they engulfed my car. I was surrounded by this crazy bunch of birds, and they were all I could see. It was as if the Lord was saying to me, "Can you see me now?

YOOHOO! I am right here!" That incident gave me peace. He saw me and He knew where I was -- on a bridge in North Platte, Nebraska.

One of the many things I love about God is that He is good, so kind and gracious. Even when I got it wrong and had crazy thought processes, He was willing to help me and to meet me where I was. He wasn't threatened by my ill-placed motives and aspirations. Instead, He set about working to bring restoration and healing in me. It wasn't overnight, and I wasn't always cooperative.

I want to encourage you, dear reader, that as long as you are moving forward and will allow Him to, God will work on you and with you. He can change your direction and motivations while teaching and transforming you in the process. God is good and He doesn't leave us to wallow in our brokenness but will do whatever it takes to make us new.

THE KIDS

What is your biggest fear? I have found that whatever it is God has a way of bringing it to the forefront and making you confront it and work through it. For me, our kids' safety has always been a source of fear. I could sit for hours and think of everything that could go wrong or happen to them, to the point that it would paralyze me. If I wasn't worrying about their safety, I was worrying about whether they would love and follow Jesus, or I was asking myself, "Are we even good parents?"

Once right after my third child, Amelia, was born, I was going through the baby blues. I kept thinking, "Why have I brought another baby into this crazy world? What was I thinking?" Over and over these thoughts would race through my mind. One evening I needed to go to the local Walmart, which was 11 miles away. As I was driving down Highway 83, I noticed there was a car coming up behind me quickly and erratically. As it was gaining on me, I had this thought to look away from it. Once it got around me, I saw a car full of unruly kids who were obviously up to no good. As I watched from behind, I could see they were acting crazy and continued driving recklessly. I followed them into town, but I slowed to put some distance between us. As I was approaching the light, it had just turned red. The car had already stopped at the light and a pickup truck sat beside them. I watched as the kids got out of their car and started circling the truck. To my shock, they took out a baseball bat and hit the hood. Inside the vehicle was a man, his wife and a young child. I was driving my husband's truck, and as I got closer, I thought to myself, "What am I going to do? Will I get a ticket if I plow into them? Could I run them over and plead postpartum depression?"

These thoughts were going through my mind as I was pulling up. I was just getting ready to rear end them when one kid moved from in front of the truck. The driver immediately ran the red light. The wild kids all jumped into their car and took off in another direction. I was left, heart racing, frothing at the mouth like a rabid dog and feeling slightly disappointed, I didn't get to run them over! I walked into the store thinking, "What was that, Lord? I told you this world was crazy; why have I brought another innocent child into it?"

He let me rant all through the store and the 11 miles home until I reached my mailbox. Then He said to my heart, "Give me your children. Didn't I warn you to look away? Didn't I make a way, so you didn't have to? Give me your kids, I can protect them just like I protected you." What could I say? He was right. I let go and found peace. God is ready willing and able to do this to every one of our fears.

One thing I learned in the early years of parenthood was to be on the lookout for teaching moments. Moments when we have the ability to make Jesus real to our kids, not just some invisible being that has no presence in everyday life. These are opportunities, and it's important to take full advantage of them no matter how trivial they might seem.

Make it real, make it simple, make it applicable. That probably was the one thing we did right. I took the Shema literally:

> Hear O Israel! The Lord our God, The Lord is one. Love the Lord your God with all your heart, with all your soul, and with all your strength. These commandments that I give you today are to be on your hearts. Impress them on your children. Talk about them when you sit at home and when you walk along the road, when you lie down and when you get up. (Deuteronomy 6: 4-7, NIV)

For that reason, our family was always talking about the Lord together. Anytime we lost something, we prayed. We praised God for beautiful sunrises and sunsets. On vacation we talked about where we saw God.

On one particular vacation, we were at SeaWorld. I was separated from the family due to a ticket mix-up and ended up sitting next to a big concrete platform alone. I was bummed. I cried out to the Lord. I wanted to sit with the rest of the family, but the seats were taken. From my vantage point I couldn't even see Shamu. I mournfully settled into my seat. It was coming to the end of the show and the trainer was looking over at where I was sitting. He then blew the whistle and Shamu flew out of the water and onto the platform right next to me! I cried. Shamu was magnificent! Can you guess what I told the kids about when it was time to share our God encounters? Never Stop talking no matter how small or big you think your God sighting is, they don't forget.

One Christmas our church was having its annual Christmas program put on by the kids, and they were having solo tryouts. Amelia wanted to sing a solo, but she was too young. She went with Kat early because we lived too far out of town for us to be running back and forth. Thus, the teachers said it was fine for her to stay with Kat while the older kids practiced. As they were trying out for solos, Amelia managed to finesse herself an audition. Later she told me she was praying she would get one.

When the day came to find out who was getting a part, she was not one of them. On the way home she was pretty upset. "It doesn't work," she said. "What doesn't work?" I asked. "Prayer," she responded. She had prayed for weeks and didn't get a solo. I felt awful for her and didn't know what to say. "Well, let's just see what happens," was the only response I could give.

A couple of weeks later the Sunday school teacher

approached me. She was going to have Amelia's class sing a particular part of a song, but for some reason the group was not getting it. Since Amelia was always there with the bigger kids, she already knew it. She was going to ask Amelia to sing it as a solo. She asked me if I wanted to tell her. I replied, "No way, you tell her."

She pulled Amelia aside and told her. Not only did she get a solo, but it was the longest solo in the whole play. Amelia was shocked. I told her, "You see Amelia, the Lord not only answered your prayer in His timing, but He answered it according to Ephesians 3:20, 'above and beyond all you could ask or imagine.'" I truly believe that God loves to answer the prayers of our children as it builds both faith and relationship. God desires relationship with our kids as much as he does with us.

I used to pray that whenever our kids were doing things that would not be pleasing to us or the Lord, He would find them out. He never failed; it seems to be another prayer the Lord loves to answer. I can remember a time when our son, Caleb, said to me, "Why would you pray that prayer?" after he was "found out" for something he had done at the time. I can't count the number of times the kids were found out by the innocent comments of others.

One of my deepest desires has been to get closer and closer to God. At the same time this very desire brought me fear and trepidation. One afternoon I was in the kitchen washing dishes. Caleb was in his room, Kat was watching PBS and Amelia was with Eric, riding the horse. I was listening to a testimony of a woman who had cancer and how she had to learn to lean on God for even the most basic of functions. She talked about how her relationship with the Lord changed and went so much deeper. As I stood there washing the dishes, I said, "Oh God, I want that so much! The desire of my heart is to walk so closely to You, but I'm afraid of the cost. What if it's to the detriment of my kids?"

I finished up the dishes and looked for Eric and Amelia out the front window, but they weren't in the arena. I asked Kat if she knew where they were, and she said that Eric had taken Amelia riding in the neighborhood.

I don't know why but it seemed like they were gone a long time. After a bit I heard the door open and Amelia came in crying, covered in dirt. She was talking about falling off the horse, but I couldn't make sense of what she was saying. After I got her cleaned up and settled her in with Kat, I went out to see Eric and find out what happened.

What he said next shook me. "You are not going to believe what happened! I put Amelia on the back of Dakota (our horse) and went out in the neighborhood. Dakota was acting like an idiot, so I went to get his attention and he reared up. Amelia tumbled off his back and ended up underneath him. The horse lifted its foot and it passed over Amelia's head -- close enough to lift up her hair. He then put it down on the other side of her head. There was nothing I could do but stand there and watch helplessly."

I turned around, ran into the house, went to my room and dropped to my knees. I thanked God for protecting my baby. I felt Him very tenderly say to me, "Give me your children. I love them more than you and I can protect them." Eric had been standing there and yet could do nothing! I gave them to Him, again. He has shown me over and over again that I cannot protect my kids. Truth is that when I started trusting Him the fear that I carried began to diminish. He is the one who is ever present. He is the one who's there watching over us even when we are sleeping.

God has many names in the Bible, and in our home, we added a few, one of those names is "God of the lost and found". I don't know about you, but, we were always losing stuff. When we did, we prayed and asked God to help us find it. It turns out God loves to answer this prayer too. Caleb had lost his wallet once when he was young; he had put all his money in it. We looked everywhere for that wallet and could not find it. We prayed and asked for the Lord's help.

Caleb went to school and I happened to be in his room. I started to look around for his wallet. As I was crawling around on the floor, I saw his art kit. We had looked around there before but this time I felt a nudge to look more carefully. When I picked it up, I could see that a part of the exterior had split apart and pulled away from its inside lining. As I looked between the two parts of the case, there was the wallet! We never would have found it, as it was so well hidden from view. The kids were as amazed as was I, and God became a little more real to them than He had been the day before. He is faithful to give us inklings that we can either ignore or be faithful to follow them through.

There is no aspect in our lives that God doesn't want to be involved in. He is always near, even when we don't perceive Him. Nothing is inconsequential to Him. When our daughter, Kathryn, was a sophomore in college, she started dating a young man. We watched our vibrant daughter withdraw from college life. Every weekend she would come home and be alone with nothing to do. Her thoughts about her future with this man—what their relationship would look like—were very disheartening. I felt my heart breaking as I envisioned their dysfunctional future. I would say to myself, "Are you kidding me? You would never agree to this crap if you were thinking clearly." What could I do? I started to pray.

I knew that if she married this guy, we would rarely get to see her. I remember one day praying for God to get rid of him. While I was in prayer, I heard in my spirit, "Do you want this relationship to end?" "Yes!" I cried. He responded: "Then step up your prayers." I started praying constantly. It wasn't long—and under the craziest set of circumstances—that Kat broke up with him. He never saw it coming.

However, we weren't out of the woods yet. He wanted her back and was going to use everything he could to do it. She was in such turmoil and heartache; she was not sure what to do. With all this happening with my daughter, I felt my own stress rising. In my head I felt like I had the storm, the whirlwind and the earthquake going on all at once. I walked outside in fear and anxiety when suddenly, in the corner of my head, I heard a whisper: "Do you trust me?" "Yes, I do, Lord," was my response. After that everything quieted down, and I knew it was all going to be ok.

Kat weathered a very difficult weekend, and on Monday she sent a text saying she was coming over. I didn't know what to expect. When she got home, I was shocked. In walked the "old" Kat. She was happy and laughing. I stood there looking at her astonished. I asked her, "Are you okay?" She said she was great. All of her friends were so happy to see her, and they told her how much she was missed. She realized how miserable and isolated she had been, and she was "over" him. After a year of hell, Kat was back. One thing I know for certain is that those prayers made the difference and turned the tide in that relationship.

ALCHOHOL AND AN EATING DISORDER

Have you ever had a sin that you cherished? One that you didn't want to give up even though it was ruining your life. I had two.

I struggled for years with drinking and bulimia. If anything set me off, that was my cue to have something to drink: not turning to the Lord but to the bottle to numb myself. I also used bulimia as a source of control when my world was chaotic. Binging and purging were one thing I thought I could control. Boy was I wrong; it wasn't long after I started binging and purging at the age of 20 that the tables turned and the thing that I thought I was controlling was controlling me.

One of the many problems with drinking was, if I had one glass of wine or cocktail, I would want another. My mood would be unpredictable; you never knew which "Rebecca" you were going to get. Would I be funny, or nasty or spoiling for a fight? Not only that, the bulimia was 10 times worse if I had been drinking. I don't think it was any coincidence that around the time of my turning 39, the Lord started to talk to me about my use of alcohol.

I had been praying and begging Him to deliver me from bulimia for some time. Whenever I would pray, however, He would bring up drinking. Every sermon I heard on the radio and everywhere I was reading in the Word kept talking about alcohol. God was after me and He wasn't going to give up. The verse that finally got me was Proverbs 23:29-35:

> Who has woe? Who has sorrow? Who has strife? Who has complaints? Who has wounds without cause? Whose eyes are red and dim? Those who linger long over wine, those who go to taste mixed wine. Do not look at wine when it is red, when it sparkles in the glass, when it goes down smoothly. At the last it bites like a serpent and stings like a viper. Your (drunken] eyes will see strange things and your mind will utter perverse things (untrue things, twisted things). And you will be (as unsteady) as one who lies down in the middle of the sea, and (as vulnerable to disaster) as one who lies down on the tip of a ship's mast, saying, "They struck me, but I was not hurt! They beat me, but I did not feel it! When will I wake up? I will seek more wine." (AMP)

How many times had I woke up with a hangover? I may not have gotten hit or beat up while I was drinking, but many times I had fallen and thought, "Wow, that didn't even hurt!" I would wake in the morning bruised, stiff and limping. I read these verses and felt such condemnation, not from God but from my own actions. When the Holy Spirit convicted me, I ran as far away from these verses as I could get.

This is where I was mentally when my brother's 40th birthday rolled around. Of course, no 40th birthday is complete without a surprise party and "the Margarita King"—a machine that makes frozen Margarita slushies. I flew to Texas to surprise him. I remember getting ready for the party when these words came to my spirit: "If you are going to drink, don't talk about me." This caution felt unnecessary and I shrugged it away.

While at the party, it wasn't long before I'd had too much to drink. Some of my brother's friends would ask me questions about my brother that I didn't think was any of their business. I would quickly respond, "Oh, hey look, there's the Margarita King," and leave to get another drink. I went and sat down by another group of my brother's friends. Among them was a man I knew to be a professing atheist. Well, of course, I had to open my big mouth and start witnessing to him about Jesus. After a while I noticed another guy get up and leave—unfazed, I continued.

The night ended, and I went back to my parents' where I slept with one foot on the floor. I woke up the next day sick as a dog and hung over. It was then I decided that I was done. I was going to quit drinking. "Lord, you win." I never said anything to anyone about my decision to quit drinking until I got home. After I flew back home, I called my mom to let her know I made it back, and that I'd decided to quit drinking.

From time to time when you make a decision to be obedient to what the Lord has been asking you to do, He has a way of cementing your decision. This was one of those times. Upon hearing the news, my mom said, "That's interesting that you say that, do you remember the guy who got up and walked away while you were talking about Jesus?" Yes, I did remember. "Well, he said you made him sick because there you were proselytizing about God and you were no different than anyone else." Ouch. I felt ill. I was so sad to have been such a poor witness for Jesus after everything He has done for me. That's when I remembered what the Holy Spirit said to me as I was getting ready for the party. I've told my kids three things to remember when they were old enough to drink: "1—Nothing will ruin your witness faster than drinking. 2—Don't talk about God when you're "drinking", He doesn't like it. 3—Make sure you're not causing anyone to stumble who may be watching you." (Of course, they all knew not to drink and drive).

After I was obedient to what He was asking me to do about drinking, the bulimia went crazy. I remember getting ready to go to a missions meeting for church when I had had yet another episode of binging and purging. I got down on my knees and said, "Lord I can't do this anymore! I'm going to be 40 years old! I am powerless to stop, please help me!" I got up, got ready and went to my meeting.

As we were getting ready to pray at the meeting, Duane, our leader, spoke to the group, "This afternoon I felt The Lord lay on my heart James 5:13-16.

> Is anyone among you in trouble? Let them pray. Is anyone happy? Let them sing songs of praise. Is anyone among you sick? Let them call the elders of the church to pray over them and anoint them with oil in the name of the Lord. And the prayer offered in faith will make the sick person well; the Lord will raise them up. If they have sinned, they will be forgiven. Therefore, confess your sins to each other and pray for each other so that you may be healed. The prayer of a righteous person is powerful and effective" (NIV).

Duane continued, "Does anyone have anything they want to say?" I felt the blood drain from my face: "You have got to be kidding me! There is no way I'm going to say what I have been doing for the last 20 years!" Being bulimic is a shameful thing. You don't broadcast it. It's a secret. I sat there thinking, "No way!" Duane kept looking at us and I was starting to sweat. I grabbed hold of my chair and hung on.

Duane said, "OK, well, if no one has anything to say..." I almost made it, but I swear the Holy Spirit threw me out of my chair because the next thing I knew I was standing on my feet in front of the group. What could I do? I confessed. I confessed to my private battle for the last 20 years— a battle that even my family didn't know about. I was mortified and embarrassed. I cried. But do you know what? They were so sweet to me. They listened with compassion. I didn't feel judged. They asked me what time of day it was when I struggled the most, and they committed to praying for me. That was it. The meeting took place and then we all went home.

After this, strange things started to happen. Beth Moore had a new Bible study out entitled, *When Godly People Do Ungodly Things*. How I interpreted the title it could have read, *When Godly People Do Ungodly Things to Me*. I signed up. Little did I know it was all about us and not about "them"! I was then asked to be in an Easter play at church. At first, I wasn't interested. But after they reassured me that I didn't have to speak, I agreed to take part in the production.

Bible study started and play practice commenced. Every Monday it was Beth Moore and every Wednesday play practice. On Mondays I was learning more and more about things that I had done to myself and to others. On Wednesdays I was put next to Peter during the part where he denies Christ. Over and over I heard Peter deny Jesus. Simultaneously, I would think to myself: "Simon, Simon—"

I couldn't remember the rest of the verse. This happened week after week.

Finally, it was Easter weekend. The play was on Friday and Saturday. As usual, I was next to Peter and, as usual, I was thinking "Simon, Simon—". Easter morning I walked into the sanctuary and sat down. When I looked up at the cross it was full of blood from the night before. I was shocked. It was like having cold water thrown on me. "Hey, they forgot to wipe off the cross," I thought to myself. Once again, those two words came to my mind: "Simon, Simon—"

Our pastor got up and preached about Peter and how, when he ran out of the courtyard, he basically left the fold (i.e. the church). Someone had to go find him and bring him back. There it was again, "Simon, Simon—" "What is that verse?"—it was driving me crazy. I looked in my concordance and there it was in Luke: "Simon, Simon, Satan has asked to sift all of you as wheat. But I have prayed for you, Simon, that your faith may not fail. And when you have turned back, strengthen your brothers" (22:31-31, NIV).

I looked at that word "when" and thought: "When? When!" Then it hit me. "Lord, you knew Simon was going to betray you. You knew he was going to leave, to run away, but you also knew he was coming back." The word "when" said it all! "Jesus you knew I was going to have this struggle, but you also knew it was going to end. You knew I would be healed and set free." In that moment, everything in me just "sat down."

When you are bulimic, everything inside you is constantly churning, and then it comes up and out. To have everything "settle" was amazing. "Lord did you just settle this? Is it over?" In my heart I knew then and there I was free. At the same time, it seemed too good to be true. I said, "Lord, you are going to have to prove this to me." We went home and celebrated Resurrection (Easter) Sunday. Monday came again and so did Bible study with Beth.

As I sat there watching the video, Beth was talking. She looked out of the TV and straight into my eyes and said, "You know, sometimes, the Lord just "settles" a thing." That was it! Sweet freedom! It was April and I was turning 40 that August. It would mark 20 years from when I started, 20 years from when I had that thought that it would be over in 20 years. It was finished, and I knew it.

It's been 15 years since that time, and I would be lying if I said that Satan hasn't tried to take me back there again. He will always try, and always check to see if any of my fences are weak. The Word says he prowls around like a roaring lion, looking for those he can devour. Stand firm against him and be strong in your faith. I'm standing firm in my declaration to him, "No, I am free!"

Dear Reader, I want you to know that anytime you gain freedom from your struggles, Satan will always try to take you back into bondage. It's what he does so, do not be surprised. Be wise to his schemes. Stand firm, even if you fall backwards. Get up and reclaim your freedom, and your surrendered ground. All is not lost, it's just a bump in the road. Who the Lord sets free is free indeed, no matter what the enemy say's.

GRATEFUL

No matter where we are or what we are doing God is always aware of us as individuals and our struggles. He is more attentive than we can ever imagine, from knowing our fears to the desires of our hearts and everything in between.

When I was a young mom, I would frequently struggle with debilitating headaches. I remember a particularly bad one; the pain wiped me out, and so I went to bed early. I remember lying there thinking about this headache and a verse came to my mind: "You do not have because you do not ask [it of God]" (James 4:2, AMP). So, I asked the Lord, "Father, please heal me of this headache." As I lay there, I realized the throbbing was gone.

I decided from that point on that I would ask the Lord for everything I needed or wanted. If I "have not because I ask not," then I am the one at fault. But if I ask and don't receive, I'm okay with that because I know God is sovereign. I can live with His "no" because I know He is a good Father, one who loves me. I can live with His decisions, yes or no He is trustworthy.

That being said, these headaches scared me. I was afraid there was something wrong and that I was going to die young. One day, feeling desperate, I told the Lord that I needed a word from Him. After praying that, I went on with my day and didn't think about it again. Do you do that? Do you ask God for something and then forget?

As I was going to sleep that night, I had this sense within my heart- not an audible voice per se, but a kind of "knowing." "Well aren't you going to look?" I was confused and caught off guard. "You asked Me for a word, but you haven't even looked for one." I got up and grabbed my Bible. The phrase that kept coming to my mind was "fear not." I flipped to Psalms 41 thinking it was the passage where this phrase was from. I opened the Word and began to read in verse 10: "So do not fear, for I am with you, do not be dismayed for I am your God. I will strengthen you and help you; I will uphold you with my righteous right hand" (NIV). I responded, "Lord I trust you but I'm afraid I'm going to die young."

In an attempt to turn the page, I ended up turning three at once. I looked down and saw chapter 46:4: "Even to your old age and gray hairs I am He, I am He who will sustain you. I have made you and I will carry you; I will sustain you and I will rescue you" (NIV). Immediately peace flooded into me, and as I looked down at what I had thought was the book of Psalms, I was shocked to see I was in Isaiah! God overrode what I thought was right and instead got me to where I needed to be. He is faithful.

God loves to delight His kids, just like we do. One afternoon while out walking, I was talking with the Lord.

It might be more accurate to say that I was doing *all* the talking. On that particular day I was telling Him how I thought some wicker furniture would look nice in our very small sunroom. That was it, I never thought much about that conversation again.

That next summer I happened to be in the furniture store in town and remembered some wicker I had seen the year before. Unfortunately, it was still way too expensive. I thought it might be marked down but it wasn't. Come August I thought I'd check it out again. I discovered that the price was significantly lower. I wasn't sure if the cost was for one piece or for all four. I asked the salesman about it and he replied, "I'm sure it's just for the couch." Then I felt the Lord nudge me, so I asked him if he wouldn't mind asking the owner. "I'm sure it's just the couch," he responded. I persisted: "If you don't mind, please just ask the owner." He wasn't happy about it, but he did.

When he came back, he looked shocked. "The owner said you can have it all at that price!" The employee quickly added, "And if you don't buy it, I am!" SOLD! On my way home I was reminded of the conversation I had with the Lord almost a year and a half earlier. "Thank you, Father!"

It amazes me how God is interested in all aspects of our lives, not just the bare necessities. His attention to both my health concerns and to the silly mussing's of my heart about a wicker couch shows just how interested He is in the details of our lives. How He delights to bless us!

THE MOVE

I once heard that God will use our dissatisfaction as a catalyst to bring about change in our lives. This was true for my family, and it all began in June of 2012. Kat was going to Spain for a Spanish immersion course associated with a group from the Seventh—day Adventist Church. Amelia and I were going to meet her in France, only it didn't turn out that way. Shortly before she was to leave for Spain, I found myself walking alone and crying out to the Lord: "Father, is this all there is? There has to be more to the Christian life than this! You promise us peace like a river, but I feel like I'm in a stagnant pond. Please tell me there is more."

I was so filled with doubt and a sense of monotony. I remember I had my phone off, but when I looked down, I saw that it was on and it was open to Hebrews 10:35. This is what I read:

> So, don't throw it all away now. You were sure of yourselves then. It's still a sure thing! But you need to stick it out, staying with God's plan so you'll be there for the promised completion. It won't be long now, He's on the way; He'll show up most any minute. (MSG)

"What?" I thought to myself. I had purposely turned my

phone off. Looking down and seeing my phone now on and reading that verse gave me tremendous hope. A hope that later, as our lives started crazily changing, gave me peace. Our lives were about to turn upside down.

Maybe a day or two later we learned that we were losing another partner in the medical group Eric was part of. Everything was up in the air. We had a big building for only two doctors. Could we make the mortgage? It was disconcerting. Amelia and I cancelled our trip to France. After the initial scare and tightening of the purse strings, we settled in to see what would happen next.

As we waited it out, we would go through periods of time without talking about the office. During these times I'd begin to think things were okay, but they weren't. Eric said we needed a contingency plan. I wasn't even sure what that meant; and I had no idea what that plan would even look like. Where would we want to live? I had no idea, but I *did* know two places we weren't going: Montana or Wyoming. That did not make my husband happy, he would have picked either.

We had talked about moving before but nothing had ever come of it, probably because I was the one pushing for it. This time, however, something was different. I started feeling like I was on a freight train and couldn't stop it. One morning I was getting ready for Bible study and listening to Christian radio, when a woman came on talking about moving from a place that she loved. She said, "Lord, you are going to have to show me you are behind this move!" I thought, "Yeah, Lord, you are going to have to show me!" Then she continued, "And do you know what the Lord did? He sold our house and it wasn't even for sale!" "Oh, heck yeah", I thought to myself.

What was crazy to me was that for years I had prayed the Lord would bring someone to our door wanting to buy our house. It never happened, so you can imagine my response to this woman's testimony— "Bring it, Lord!" I went to Bible study after the radio program was over. That very day one of the ladies pulled me aside and said, "Hey, we hear you might be moving." I was shocked. Our situation wasn't public knowledge. She could tell by the look on my face that I didn't know what to say. She quickly added, "Don't worry, we won't say anything. But if you think you are moving, we know someone who would buy your house without a realtor."

I about fainted. "Lord, what are you doing here?" I was scared, but I had the distinct feeling He was laughing. I gave my friend my phone number and said she could pass it along. A day later, the phone rang, and her friend came over to look. A couple days after that, they called and said, "We want to buy your house. We don't care when you leave. When you are ready, we will be too." And that was that! I guess we were moving.

We started earnestly looking at places we would like to move. Oddly enough, when Kat had come home from Spain, she had met some kids who were attending Walla Walla University, and she wanted to go to school there. We did not like the idea: "No, you are not going to a college based on where a handful of kids that you met on a summer trip are going to school." But strangely enough, that is exactly where my husband started looking. Washington state! Are you kidding? We had never even thought of vacationing in Washington.

The train just kept chugging along, and it was gaining speed. It was rapidly becoming apparent that we were going to be leaving. My heels in the sand were doing nothing to slow it down. God was firmly closing all doors in North Platte and opening them in Washington.

Looking back, I am totally amazed. We started thinking about moving in November and after calling around, we began the interview process in March. We interviewed in four places, and Walla Walla was the first place we looked. All roads kept leading back there. We finally settled on Walla Walla. You will never guess what the name of the hospital and clinic were: "Providence."

God can be so funny, yet not funny, all at the same time. Kat said to me, "Hey, since you are looking at Walla Walla, why can't I look at Walla Walla University?" Why not indeed? Another big surprise! Kat chose to attend college in Walla Walla. Amelia was there by default, and Caleb was much closer than before at the University of Montana in Missoula. I used to wonder if we ended up in Walla Walla because we told Kat, "No." But as I look back, and can now see the whole picture, the Lord had something for all of us.

It's exciting to move, and I was caught up in all the hustle and bustle. God even had His hand in where we would live. We were having a hard time finding a place, so I'd get on the Internet every day and see if anything new came up. Finally, I saw this house on the Internet and I just knew that it was "the place." But when we looked at it, the sellers wouldn't come down much on the price, so we moved on and decided to build.

We put money down on a lot, found a builder and a plan. It eventually fell through. We had different ideas from the builder, and we backed out. We needed to find a place. We called the owners of the house back, made an offer and they accepted. We bought the house the Lord had shown us months before. I was amazed that in such a hot market it was still available. I later learned that in North Platte, Amelia "threw a fleece out" to the Lord and said, "If this move is of you, would you give me a room with a window seat?" God answered that prayer asked in faith. She got a room with two window seats—only God! I was getting excited.

Once we were all settled into our home in Walla Walla, what had at first seemed like a great move started to feel more like a nightmare. If I had thought Eric's work in North Platte had long hours, here it was worse, much worse. In

North Platte Eric could bring his work home but in Walla Walla he literally was at the office from 6:30 a.m.—10:00 p.m. Thank God for some great neighbors who took me under their wings and got me out of the house from time to time. Otherwise, it was just Amelia and I, and she was gone all day at school and had hours of homework at night. Little did I know that this was right where God wanted me, and He had my full attention. God had healing in mind for me, and I didn't even know I had a problem.

The first lesson I learned was about friendship. I left my best friend Ellen behind when we moved from North Platte. She is the closest thing I have to a sister; she is that friend that Proverbs 18:24 talks about. I am convinced that if it weren't for Ellen, Eric and I would have gotten a divorce long ago. We became family. She filled in the gaps of the long hours I otherwise would have been alone while Eric was at work.

The Lord also showed me how I had taken her and a whole group of friends for granted. How could I have thought that leaving my home of 20 years could be easy? After the move I realized just how much I really relied on Ellen and my friends for life, laughter and tears. Friends who were there through good and bad times. It wasn't until I was without them that I began to ask myself, "Who am I going to lean on in the empty nest years?" They were quickly bearing down on me. Who is going to be there to tell me that it will get better while handing me a Kleenex?" It's those lifelong friendships that give your life color and flavor, through which you know and are known. Don't take them for granted. I had none of that in Walla Walla. I didn't know what I had until it was gone.

Instead, I had been so excited. I thought for sure this was going to be my big break. I was going to Walla Walla as a missionary! I was convinced the people there needed me. I was going to start a ministry, lead Bible studies, "me, me, me!" I could not have been more wrong. My plan and God's plan did not line up and one of them had to go. Any guess as to whose?

I had things in my life that had to go. Things like pride, selfishness and vainglory; things that, at the time, I didn't even know were an issue until God got me alone. I remember like it was yesterday, being in our local grocery store and crying out to the Lord: "Father I don't even hear my name anymore." He said, "I know." Ouch! I got the point. In North Platte, my reputation and my name had gone hand and hand. That's when I realized how much "being known" meant to me. I stood there looking pride right in the face, and I realized that face was mine. That was just the beginning. God was getting ready to take it down to the studs. One thing to remember is that in the pain of growth, God always dishes it up with plenty of grace and mercy.

I found that grace and mercy in one of the most heart breaking and trying times in my life to date. It was around this time that Eric, Amelia and I were planning on going back to Nebraska for a wedding. After the celebration, Amelia and I were going to head to North Platte for a couple of weeks. I was going to stay with Ellen, and Amelia was going to camp with her best friend, Kelly. After camp we were going to Denver to visit my brother, Rob, for a week.

We had a great time at the wedding and got a ride to North Platte with friends. While on the way I received a text from my mom saying my brother had been in a terrible motorcycle accident, and they didn't know if he was going to make it. God is amazing. There I was, I just "happened" to be in Nebraska and just "happened" to have two weeks before we had to leave. Our friends took me straight to the airport. Because the plane was late, one seat became available. I caught that flight, got to Denver, picked up a rental car and got to the hospital almost seamlessly, and in record time.

Does anything prepare you for seeing a loved one in a hospital bed hooked up to a ventilator and a sundry of various machines? I have worked in a hospital as an X-ray technician and a nurse, but I was not prepared for my brother. I still see him there, and I'm reminded that God is and was good. From the outside, Rob looked surprisingly good. His injuries from the crash were not life threatening in and of themselves. He had broken ribs and road rash. What none of us knew was that he had pulmonary hypertension, and when they loaded him up with fluids in the ER he crashed. He was alone when I got there, but I knew he realized it when I walked in because he wrinkled up his brow.

They had given my brother medications to paralyze him to help his body heal so he couldn't even open his eyes. My nephew, Taylor, came in and was devastated. At hearing his son cry, Rob's blood pressure went way up, so they put him in a deeper coma.

My mom arrived from Dallas and we settled in for the long haul. As I look back, I remember this time to be the worst of times and the sweetest of times. God met us there. Rob's friends began to trickle in as they heard the news. To see big, grown men cry unashamed was such a gift to us. Just to see how much he was loved by others was beautiful. It gave us such peace.

We had so many great visits with his friends, and the hospital staff was awesome. We were amazed at how many hospital employees went to his same church.

In the meantime, Amelia was done with camp and we needed to get her to Denver. It turned out that there was an undercover agent from the United Kingdom visiting North Platte. He was teaching about Internet crime and was going to the Denver airport the next day. He heard about our plight from friends and offered to bring Amelia to Denver the next morning. It was all arranged that they would meet at a local hotel and go from there.

Our friend Kevin took her to introduce them. Thankfully so, because the detective had an intimidating appearance. Amelia would have been freaked out when she first met him if Kevin had not been there. Once again, God had a divine encounter set up for the two of them.

Amelia talked about the Lord to this man for four hours, sharing everything she had learned at camp. When they got to Denver, he asked her what book she recommended for him to read besides the Bible because he had a hard time understanding it. She just happened to have a copy of *Mere Christianity* by C.S. Lewis that she had been toting around for forever, hoping to have time to read, but never did. She gave it to him, and he told her she had helped him overcome some of his cynical views of Christians and Christianity.

I picked her up at Denver International Airport and took her to the hospital. The next couple of days were a blur except that, every 12 hours, like clockwork, Rob would crash and a medical team would have to fight to bring him back.

Sunday rolled around and it was Father's Day. We needed a break, so we decided to go to Rob's church. It was a great service. I felt that the Lord said he was going to heal Rob, so I couldn't wait to get back to the hospital and pray for him.

Once we got there, I laid my hand on Rob's heart and prayed for God's healing. A couple of hours later, like clockwork, Rob crashed again. The nurses came in to manually ventilate him. It seemed like it was taking longer than usual, so we stepped out. I didn't think anything of it because I knew he was going to be healed.

The nurses were in there for what seemed like forever, and finally one came out and said, "I think he is dying!" WHAT?! That can't be! Not only did I feel that I had gotten a promise from God, but my nephew wasn't at the hospital and our other brother was on the way from the airport.

On the phone my nephew begged me to keep him alive until he could get there. In the meantime, the doctor who was working with Rob had just gone home. I asked that they keep trying for these reasons, and the resident who had been assigned to Rob started yelling at me—telling me how selfish and inhumane I was. I didn't know what to do, I was so stressed. All I could think was, "Oh God!"

The next thing I knew Rob's doctor came back and started running the code. Rob was soon stabilized. My brother and nephew both got there and were able to go in and spend time with him. I asked the doctor what made him come back, and he said he just felt like he needed to return. After some time, the doctor came in to talk to us and explain that there really wasn't anything else they could do for Rob. They were maxed out on the ventilator and all the drugs they had been using to keep him alive. He told us that there were worse things than dying. He talked to my mom and told her she needed to make the decision because Rob was her son and it was getting harder and harder to bring him back. His body was shutting down.

Meanwhile, I was thinking, "Lord! What is going on? You said you were going to heal him!" No answer. After much discussion, we decided to take him off the ventilator. My family members said they could not be there to watch, and the doctor felt it should be me since I was a nurse and had seen people die before. What he didn't know was I was only a nurse for a few months before I got pregnant. So, not really. I went in. As they were getting him ready, I put my head on his chest and talked softly to him. I told him how much I loved him, and I wouldn't leave him. I prayed that the Lord would be merciful and that he wouldn't suffer.

It was so strange and surreal, I could hear the heart monitor beeping and getting slower—then suddenly, he was gone. I just knew he had flown away. It was like a butterfly, something just lifted off of him and I could feel he had left, though the heart monitor was still continuing to slow. The nurse told the rest of the family to come in because it was so peaceful, but I knew he was already gone.

I found it interesting that in life we never had someone we called dad, we didn't celebrate Father's Day but God, He took him home to be with Him, his heavenly father, to tangibly be in His presence on Father's Day. That was no accident or coincidence, that was God.

Rob was cremated and the funeral was set for July. Rob's death opened a lot of doors for conversations everywhere

I went. I think it was part processing and part my desire to see something good come out of Rob's passing. As I pondered his death, one thing became very clear to me. I was so touched by how many people loved Rob that I remember thinking to myself, "I want that. I want to be loved like Rob."

Walking through that time with my brother is one that I wouldn't want to repeat with anyone, but I know, without a shadow of doubt, that I would not have to walk it alone. He (God) would be there to guide and give comfort. God was tangibly with us every step and as I look back, I can see His hand of mercy all over us.

For the next three years I battled with the Lord over what I had done wrong. Had I given up too soon? Should I have prayed more? Did I not have enough faith? Basically, I was asking, "Did I kill my brother by doing something wrong or by not doing enough?"

It wasn't until I was in Impact class through my church that I got my answer. It came from the Book of Esther. Mordecai was talking to Esther and telling her that if she doesn't go to the King for the Jews, that help *would* come but not from her. She herself would perish just like the rest of them. That's when I realized something: even if I was short a prayer, with all the care givers there who went to his church, someone would have stepped up to pray for him. I don't think God is so cruel that He would say, "Oh, only if you prayed one more time," or "you just didn't have enough faith." How would you know how much faith was enough? God talks about mustard seed faith. As I pondered this kind of faith, I realized that a mustard seed is hardly anything. Mustard seed faith is asking; it's looking up. The Word says that Jesus is "the Author and Perfecter of faith" (Hebrews 12:2, AMP). The Lord showed me that even if I hadn't prayed enough, help was there, and someone would have prayed. It just wasn't His plan.

If any of you are struggling with guilt that you could have or should have done more, leave it with God and trust in His goodness and character. It's a choice I had to make, and it has brought me peace.

TIME FOR A CHANGE / THE SHIFT

Time passed and seasons changed, and the Lord would give to me lessons here and there but nothing earth-shattering. By my own stubborn will, I became numb to those things God wanted to work on. That was until Kat found Life Church Walla Walla. She was not satisfied where she was and, quite frankly, none of the rest of us were either.

Satan knows how to lull you to sleep and keep you complacent. But right before my eyes my daughter and her faith were being transformed, and I was getting very uncomfortable. I then went from being uncomfortable to downright angry. What was going on here?

She started talking about prophetic words, and Impact class and serving more. She started talking about all the things God was telling her through the prophetic words of other people and in my spirit, I was thinking, "This is not God, God doesn't do those things anymore! That's all fine and good, but don't get your hopes up." What was interesting to me was that God had his hand over my mouth, and there was very little He would let me say out loud. I could feel His restraining arm on me. By now I was seething. I started to unravel and what was on in the inside of me rose to the surface and it was ugly.

I tried to squash Kat quickly, and I really hurt her

feelings. I felt so bad that I started back-pedaling so that we could be friends again. We weathered that storm in a kind of uneasy truce and I limped away while she skipped off to join the class at Life Church called Impact.

I started to see a change in her. It was like seeing the joy of her salvation restored. Jesus had gotten a face-lift and it looked good on Kat. One weekend while we were gone, Kat took Amelia to Life Church with her. Amelia came back bug-eyed! She told me when we got back that she was shocked by what she heard. She was like, "Wait, What?" They were talking about the Holy Spirit, and she was amazed.

Francis Chan wrote a book called *The Forgotten God* and that pretty much sums up my experience with Him. The Holy Spirit is a person. One who is not often talked about in a lot of churches. I wonder if it's because He doesn't fit in the "box" we often put Him in. He also has a tendency to bring about change and that makes us very uncomfortable.

Therefore, hearing and seeing people at Life Church who were so familiar with His Spirit made me uneasy. Eric and I began going with Kat because she really wanted us to try it. I really liked it a lot. The people were excited to be there. It felt alive and engaging, but we were a part of another church at the time. Amelia was entrenched in the youth ministry and I helped with it as well. We settled back into the familiar and would step out on occasion and visit Life Church with Kat.

In 2016 Amelia graduated and went to Wheaton College in Illinois. Eric and I started attending Life Church more regularly. We would go there on Saturday nights and to our church on Sundays. It was at this time when Kat left for Youth with a Mission (YWAM) and Caleb was living and working in Montana, that Eric started having crazy dreams that were very self-deprecating and depressing. One Saturday night the pastor was talking about spiritual warfare, and Eric knew, judging from his dreams, that he was in it. He raised his hand for prayer and after that I don't think we ever went back to our old church.

Now that we were fully committed, the subject of the Impact class kept coming up. I thought to myself, "I would never do that. Why would I? I have been studying the Bible for years. No way." What is it with the Lord? As soon as you say an emphatic "no" you can almost guarantee He is going to have the last word and it's going to be "yes."

This time was no exception. Kat returned home in April, and there was a welcome-back party for her. Eric and I went. While there the conversation switched to Impact and people were talking about who was going to be in it. As if by a ventriloquist I announced, "I am going to apply."

What?! Where did that come from? It was as if the Lord slipped it in when I wasn't looking. Then I heard Eric say he was, too! Are you kidding me? There were way too many people around to back out now. We were committed.

Up to that point, Eric and I were struggling. He had

been working such long hours and it was starting to take its toll. It wasn't as bad as it had been, but it wasn't good. It was like we were standing back-to-back and facing in different directions, we were close, but not going down the same path.

I don't know about you, but I want my marriage to be all that God says it can be. And we were far from it. So, by Eric saying he was going to take the class, I had hope.

I'm not going to say it was easy or that things changed overnight, but it was a start. This is what I know about God, He is good, and He doesn't let go. He will move heaven and earth to get us to where we need to be. He doesn't get overwhelmed or discouraged when we don't comply or dig our heels in. Instead He continues to gently, and sometimes not so gently, prod us along towards growth and healing.

PART 2

HEARING WHEN I KNEW TO LISTEN

THE PRE-GAME: GETTING READY FOR IMPACT

It's funny to me that even before we started Impact, God decided to get a jump on the lessons. I believe He was building excitement in me for what was to come.

I was listening to Randy Alcorn on the radio one day. He was speaking about "treasure in heaven." I've never really thought much about treasure. I mean, I knew I wanted it, who doesn't? But what is it really? At first, I thought it was wealth in some form or another. However, I knew it wasn't gold or precious stones because Scripture tells us those are building materials in heaven.

After listening to Randy, I felt so silly. He talked about his family members and loved ones as treasure. That's when it hit me: "Hello! People are the treasure! Everyone!" Our desire should be that everyone we meet be in heaven with us. Good news is meant to be shared. As I thought about this, I realized I wanted as many people with me as possible.

Seeing people as my treasure has changed my whole perspective on storing up treasure in heaven. God let me sit on that thought for a while before deepening my perspective. He woke me in the middle of the night and brought this idea to mind once more: "where your treasure is, there your heart will be also" (Matthew 6:21, NIV). I wondered, "what else is there that's more important than people?" Boom—it hit me. It's Him!

God is the treasure. If He is my treasure then all things flow from that point: His authority over my life, my obedience in all things, my giving, my loving, my serving. It all flows from one source—Him. The thing about treasure is that it usually comes with a map. As I pondered this, I realized that we, as Christians, have been given a treasure map: God's Word. It teaches us everything we need to know about the prize we seek. I began to think about 2nd Corinthians 4:7-9, which talks about treasure: "But we have this treasure in jars of clay…" (NIV). We are the "jars" which contain the Holy Spirit. The great paradox of it all is that He is both treasure and map: when He is in our lives, He leads us on the journey He has already planned for us.

Getting this epiphany was the beginning of God prying open my tightly fisted hands; He loosened my grip and exposed the counterfeit gods I had held dear. I started to study Matthew 6:19-21 and began to see both people and my possessions differently.

I don't know about you but there are certain passages in the Bible I struggle with. Passages I felt were foundational, but just couldn't completely grasp. One of these passages was the "Beatitudes". I was never quite sure what Jesus meant when He said that the people were blessed when they were poor, or meek, or in mourning… So, I set about understanding what He was saying, what He was trying to tell me, as I took my time to understand. I started reading "The Sermon on the Mount," in Matthew 5. I was jolted out of my thoughts when I felt Jesus talking to me. In these verses Jesus says: "Blessed are the poor in spirit...Blessed are those who mourn...Blessed are the meek... Blessed are those who hunger and thirst for righteousness...Blessed are the pure in heart...Blessed are the peacemakers..." (Matthew 5:3-9, NIV). As I read this, I was reminded of the account in Luke and remembered it being somewhat different. I turned to Luke 6. In this account, Jesus is standing in the midst of the multitude. The people are touching Him, power is going out from Him and people are being healed. He, however, is looking at His disciples and teaching them saying, "Look around you, look at these people." Can you just see Him gesturing at those around Him who are touching Him, believing Him for a miracle? They are the poor in spirit, they are mourning, they are weeping, they are meek, they are hungry, they are merciful and pure in heart. They are persecuted. They are downtrodden, they are blind, lame and possessed—the lowest of the low. They are all there milling around Him. Jesus is standing in the middle of humanity: they are touching Him, and power is going out of Him.

You can almost see the sparks fly. As I read this account, I saw His head swing around and look directly at me as if I were there. He was teaching and showing me! He was telling me, "Look, it's because of these things that the people are coming to me. That is why they are "blessed," because they NEED me." They found the answer, and power was flowing from Him to them—and it can to us too!

Jesus shows us that life is messy, and we are going to get our hands dirty as His disciples. You see, I like to stand far off from people. I hold out my Subway gift cards and say, "Here you go, be fed and well." Jesus challenged me on this: "No, that's not enough! Get in there, let people touch you and you be me to them. Let them touch you; love them for me. That's when my power flows, and that's how you begin to break down the walls around your heart."

After teaching me this lesson, the Holy Spirit reminded me of a time when our kids were young. My mom was visiting from Texas, and we were going to Applebee's for lunch. The day was freezing and there was a strong north wind blowing. I saw a homeless man walking, hunkered down against the cold and a blanket around his shoulders. His pants were too short, and he didn't have socks on. I felt a nudge from the Holy Spirit. I told him magnanimously to come in, and I would pay for his lunch, anything he wanted. The hostess put him at a table with his back to us. As I sat with my family enjoying their company, all I could really see was this homeless man's back as he sat alone.

At the time I patted myself on the back for paying for his lunch. I fed him, but I did nothing for his soul. Unlike Jesus, I didn't let him near me. I didn't treat him as if he were precious in God's sight, and I have never forgotten. I haven't done much if all I have done is feed him but have done nothing for his soul.

The summer before Impact, I was asked if I would be interested in joining the board of the Christian Aid Center (CAC). I love the CAC. It is so much of what is dear to my heart: women, children and freedom. My desire is for women to find freedom in Christ. The women who stay at the center have had so many setbacks, heartbreaks and abuse. I know there is an answer to every one of their hurts, pains and addictions. It's Jesus and His love.

At first when I was asked to be on the board I thought, "Wow, they want me!" But it turns out this was God at work answering my prayers before I even knew to ask (see Isaiah 65:24). After joining the board, I decided it would be good for me to take some of the classes that the organization offered to women so I could speak more knowledgably about what the CAC does. It wasn't until my second year in Impact that I actually had the chance to take some classes.

I ended up in a class called "ACE Overcomers" created by Dave Lockridge. ACE stands for Adverse Childhood Experiences. It is a common tool used by health care workers and mental health specialists to diagnose children who have been raised in adverse circumstances. The higher your score the more likely you are to have myriad of psychiatric and social issues including a much higher propensity towards committing suicide. "ACE Overcomers is a unique ministry that blends powerful biblical principles with sound science. To overcome addiction, anger, and depression, you must strike at the root of the problem. How do you respond to the stressors of life? By faith, and by trusting God or by seeking relief through self-medicating with drugs, tobacco, or alcohol? Dave teaches how to retrain your brain, reset your nervous system, and discipline your spirit to be the new you." (Citation). This was the first class I found myself in at the CAC. I thought I ended up in this class by chance, but then I remembered that with God, there is no such thing as chance, instead He had more healing in mind for me.

We began the class by taking the ACE's test. I was shocked that I scored a 5 out of 10—10 being the worst. Dave started to explain what these scores meant in detail. As he was talking, I saw myself in his words. For the first time in my life I understood why I have responded in the ways that I did: why I thought the way I did and where I got stuck over and over again. Then he said something that that gave me hope. He said that I didn't have to think that way; I can learn to think differently. With all the information about neuroplasticity we now know we have the power to change the shape of our brains, and we can think differently. "Wow!" As I sat there looking around the room I realized that—while I might not be a resident of the center—the only thing that separated me from these women was that, somewhere in our pasts, I made a left where they made a right or vice versa. Since that first session, I have learned to speak differently to myself and recognize triggers that set me up for failure. One day I asked the Lord, "How did I end up in that class?" He impressed upon me that I had asked for it. "When did I ask for that?" He responded: "When you prayed in your prayer language." That worked for me—I would have never known to pray for that.

IMPACT

At this point, summer was coming to an end and Impact was looming ahead of me. I remember feeling at first like it was chasing after me. Then, after a little while, it seemed like I was being pulled toward it. As we got closer to the start date, however, it felt like it would never come. For me, I felt like this was a last-ditch effort for healing in more areas than I wanted to count. I kept asking, "Lord are you going to show up?" But found no answer.

Just before Impact started our nephews and my mother came to visit for a couple of weeks. As was to be expected, my mom and I had our usual knock-down, drag-out fight over the same old things. It got so heated that it was up in the air as to whether my mom would stay or go home early. We cooled off and were able to get along to finish out the trip.

I find it interesting how the Lord sometimes speaks to me. He will continually highlight examples in my life that communicate a message until I finally get it. He showed me up close in people whom I love dearly what unforgiveness looks like. After watching people I love participate in painful and frustrating exchanges followed by "I'm sorry," It dawned on me that we can say we are sorry all we want, but if there is no forgiveness we will remain in a vicious cycle forever. I said this to the Lord and felt Him say, "I know, right?!"

I thought that was a weird response. I pondered this for a while, and it hit me. That is exactly what I have been doing to my mom. To drive the message even closer to home, my pastor was preaching a series on forgiveness at this time.

Isn't it funny how the Lord orchestrates the circumstances in our lives? My mother has apologized so many times to me over the years for things in my past, but I had not forgiven her. Wow! I had some work to do. God was on the move and getting me ready for a big breakthrough.

Hope takes many forms and for me one of them was Impact. It was here! The day that I'd fought against, then dreaded, and finally anticipated, had arrived. It's funny how a class at church can bring forth such visceral responses—yet it does, and for very good reasons. For me, Impact made me dig deep, look for areas of a hardened heart, look for where I'd left the path, and look at where I have had wrong thoughts about the Godhead.

For someone who was raised in the church and studied the Bible, I didn't know much about God: I didn't know how He loved me just as I am, how He saw me as perfect, or about the obedience He desires from me. Don't get me wrong, I memorized these things, but I didn't *know* these things experientially. It hadn't travelled the eleven inches from my head to my heart. But I was about to find out, and so much more.

The first day of Impact was nerve-wracking. We were

all so nervous. Our class consisted of people representing a variety of ages and walks of life—some were single, some married and some divorced. What we had in common was we were tired of the status quo, we were all hungry for more of God, and we all wanted to see and be a part of God at work.

My verse for as long as I can remember has been Habakkuk's prayer: "Lord, I have heard of your fame; I stand in awe of your deeds, Lord. Repeat them in our day" (3:2, NIV). My own addition to this prayer has been that I would be a part of these deeds in my own day: "Oh God, let me be a part! I want to see you big, God!" I want people to see that there is a God in heaven, and He is amazing! He loves them and He still does miracles. These are the lessons I learned as I was learning to listen.

God started out with a bang. Pastor Bob had started a series on forgiveness. I asked the Lord if there was someone I needed to forgive, and He said nothing. I thought, "Hmmm I'm good." About a week later, as I was taking a bath, a face flashed before me. Someone I hadn't thought of in years, not since I was at least 13. The man who abandoned my family. I was shocked.

Then I remembered the series from church on forgiveness. Thank you, Holy Spirit. As I thought about this man, I realized that I couldn't bring myself to forgive him. I started to pray about it, and this is what it finally came down to. “Lord, even though I don’t feel like it, but because you said so, I forgive him.” That was that. I realized then that God doesn’t ask for 100 percent, He asks for what we have and meets us there.

After that, I felt like the Lord wanted me to write a letter to this man telling him I forgave him. Geeze! OK Lord. The beauty of the Internet and social media, I was able to locate him without much trouble. I messaged him telling him I forgave him. I did not hear back from him.

At this time, in Impact, we were meeting with our leaders one-on-one to discuss the Lord, our feelings and what was going on in our lives. As I was walking into the restaurant to meet my leader, I got a ping from Messenger on my phone. It was him. WOW! It had been weeks. I read his response before I went into the restaurant. He was so glad I had messaged him. He thought of us often, he felt bad for us, and he had tried to find us. So, when I sat down with my leader, his response was fresh on my mind. Our conversation led me to telling Connie, my Impact leader, that I “trusted” in Jesus but didn’t *really* trust Him. She asked in response, “Why do you think that is?”

Then with all this stuff fresh on my mind it hit me like a ton of bricks. Why would God let that happen to us? God knew what was going to happen and how it was going to change the trajectory of our lives. Nothing would ever be the same—our relationships, even between each other, would be different. I said all this to Connie and when I had finished, I heard Him say as clear as day, "Because it was wrong!"

Oh my gosh! It was wrong. Everything about his connection to us was wrong. He never should have come with our family in the first place. The Lord didn't let the relationship continue because it wouldn't have been right. In a snap, all my fear and anxiety dissipated. The baggage I had carried everywhere just fell to the ground. For the first time I felt confidence in the Lord. I understood how Shadrach, Meshach and Abednego, in Daniel 3:18 could say, "Even if our God doesn't save us, we will not bow to you King Nebuchadnezzar." Got it! I *could* trust Him.

Assurance of God's faithfulness flowed through me. Even though the man had left us long ago, I finally knew that God had been protecting us. Even though hard, it was so much better than if things had remained as they were, for both sides.

Because of this revelation and the peace it gave me, I wanted to remember this moment. I decided to tattoo the words "Even If" on my right wrist. It has since been a great tool for testifying to others about the faithfulness of God, even in the most difficult of circumstances. And even when I had no perception of His presence.

All of this would have been enough, but God was not done. You see, I struggled so much with discontentment and with an aversion to living in the moment. I had no idea where that came from. No matter what we were doing, I was always waiting for the next thing. I couldn't even enjoy vacations because I was always waiting for them to get over so I could move on to what was next.

Looking back, I think subconsciously I was always waiting for something bad to happen. I guess the Lord thought, "Well as long as we are here let's not leave behind any loose ends." I started pondering, "Why do I have such a hard time enjoying the present?" I started thinking about our being abandoned and how terrible that time was. I coped by putting my head down and getting through it. "Just keep your eyes focused ahead. If you keep your head down, maybe you will escape with minimal pain."

Once we got to Colorado all those years ago, it wasn't long until my mom figured out, she couldn't make it on her own. I was sent to California to live with my uncle, who was pretty much a stranger to me. That was hard, and so I kept my head down and focused on just getting through it, eyes fixed on the day I could go back home. When I returned, my mom married a man who—within a month—became verbally and sometimes physically abusive. "Put your head down, focus on the future and just get through it"—this had become my mantra.

Not long after high school, I got married to get out of the house. I tried to call off the wedding, but I wasn't strong enough. Once again, I put my head down and focused on the future. In less than a year, we divorced. It was devastating, so I put my head down. As I look back, I am reminded of how you can take breadcrumbs and make a trail into a box trap. A pigeon will follow the trail all the way into the trap, never looking up or from side to side. All you have to do is pull the string and "boom," it is trapped.

I was that pigeon. I had walked right into Satan's trap, and I never heard the slamming door. I prayed and asked the Holy Spirit to help me find the root. He did, and from there I was able to weed it out and look at the present differently. Since that time, I am learning how to focus on the present and enjoy it. I am truly amazed how I will struggle forever trying to figure out this problem or that, for months even. Then when I take a moment and ask God, the answer is usually not long in coming. Oh, that I would ask sooner rather than later!

THE FAST

In the middle of Impact, Life Church Walla Walla does a fast to give the Lord the "first fruits" of the year. This happens in January. We do this fast in order to hear the Lord and get our hearts right before Him. We intercede on behalf of our church, our community and our lives. I had been fasting and praying once a week for our kids for years, but this time I was going to do it for me too. I claimed Psalm 51:10 and 12, "Create in me a clean heart, O God, and renew a right spirit within me...Restore to me the joy of your salvation and uphold me with a willing spirit" (ESV).

There were so many things I wanted to have broken off me—areas I wanted breakthrough, which included direction for my family. But if I'm being totally honest, the fast was mostly for myself. I wanted God to show up and untangle the knots inside of me. I wanted the Lord to break off a slave mentality that kept me in bondage to an addictive personality. I wanted Him to kill off the fear of being invisible and the desire to be seen. Last but not least, I desired Ezekiel 36:26 for myself: "And I will give you a new heart and put a new spirit in you; I will remove from you your heart of stone and give you a heart of flesh" (NIV). I felt deep inside me a kind of hardness I could not seem to break off. These were the desires of my heart and I was going all in. For the next 40 days I fasted solid food. I had water for the first seven days, then water and broth until I hit the 20-day mark, and then added one smoothie a day until day 40. I'm not going to lie—I was scared. From where I stood in the beginning, it looked daunting. I had never tried anything like it before, but I was desperate.

On the seventh day of the fast I had a dream that I was in Impact class and our leader asked me to pray. At first, I was praying, "Lord please do this and please do that." But as I continued, my prayer changed and became more forceful. When I started praying with boldness and confidence, I heard the Lord say in my dream, "Who are you talking to?" I realized then that it was Him, my Father. I felt Him nudge me to start praying with confidence: prayers befitting a daughter and not a slave, prayers to a good Father who loves me.

The very next day, the Lord began showing me how to make His Word my stronghold. I give Satan way too much leverage and credit. God is my rock, and His words are the firm ground on which I stand. Satan is a master of smoke and mirrors. He makes things that aren't real appear real; He uses our fears to render us ineffective.

On day ten of the fast, I was reading about Absalom, the son of King David. In 2 Samuel 15, it describes how Absalom would stand near the city gate. As people went to see King David, Absalom would step out and call to them. He would ask about their troubles and hand out advice before they ever made it to the king. Thus, he stole the hearts of the people.

As I read those words, I was cut to the heart. I used to do that very thing at Bible study. As my friends were on the way to the Lord, I'd step out and speak to them about their troubles. I'd hand out advice rather than have them seek the Lord for an answer for themselves. As I looked back at this, I was heartsick. I hated that I had been more of a hindrance than a help. I had usurped God's position and stolen His glory, instead of encouraging them to foster a deeper relationship for themselves.

During the 40 days, the Lord also gave me a vision. I was up praying at 3 a.m. when, suddenly, I felt like I was in a very large and dark space. When I looked up, I saw a line of floodgates as far as the eye could see. The atmosphere was one of anticipation and expectancy—as if the room was holding its breath. In the background I could hear the "drip, drip, drip" of water and the creaking of straining metal. "What Lord, will open the floodgates?" I asked. Not long ago I received my answer… Belief.

On January 26, day 12 of the fast, Kat was giving a speech during chapel at the college she attended. It was during the student-led week of worship. It was an open forum, so anyone could attend. As Kat was preparing for her testimony, she would read it to me. The first draft was witty and well-written, but I couldn't help thinking the students wanted to hear more about who she was. The second draft, while better, still felt more like a speech. Since the student body had voted for her to speak, I felt the students wanted to know about Kat.

What she ended up with was beautiful – no script, just an outline. Monday came and the first speaker had a great speech. It was polished to perfection. It was clever, funny, had perfect cadence and the speaker even had audience participation. This was the kind of speech I would have been tempted to give—I would have wanted to "wow the crowd." Kat, however, got up and shared from her heart. It was amazing! The difference was obvious.

While watching Kat, God taught me what Paul meant when he said, "And my message and my preaching were very plain. Rather than using clever and persuasive speeches, I relied only on the power of the Holy Spirit" (1st Cor. 2:4, NLT). You see, I love speaking, and when I think about what I want to say I generally think of "wowing the crowd." I want to show the audience what I've got and make them laugh.

God showed me that day that this kind of speaking isn't a demonstration of His power but mine. What people want and need are not flowery words but the plain and simple truth. The end result is they get their eyes off us and on Jesus. This was a much-needed lesson for me.

On day 30 of my fast, I was at church when I realized

that I'd lost the diamond out of my wedding ring. After church was over, I was talking to my daughter when she looked down and said, "Mom, where is your diamond?" I had a strange sense of calm. Looking at my wedding ring was like looking into child's mouth who had just lost a front tooth.

We went to where I was sitting and started looking all around my seat. Kat went to look in the church kitchen and in the trash. With the help of my friend, Theresa, we added about 20 people to the hunt. I was somewhat embarrassed because I just knew it would be found. I was so certain that I was ready to tell all our lookers to go home. I knew that if we couldn't find it that day, the cleaners would the next.

Just as we were about to call it off, my friend Maggie walked up to me and said, "Now what are we looking for? I replied: "The diamond from my wedding ring." She asked where I had been sitting and I showed her. She immediately looked down and said, "There it is." She was so calm and matter of fact. And there it was! God had given me a supernatural dispensation of faith.

This same type of situation had happened to me twice before – once when we lost Kat at an amusement park and once when I lost my grandmother's pearls. At the time, I knew I would find those pearls, even though I had no idea how. They turned up three years later. These instances are a "setup for a step up" in our faith, when God takes us to a greater level of trust in Him.

After the fast was over, as a sort of wrap-up, I went with Kat to a "Jesus Encounter" in Grandview, Washington. It was held by my friend Sheila Stutzman at the church where she and her husband pastor called Remnant House.

The entire weekend was incredible. We worked through strongholds, soul ties, and unforgiveness—just to name a few. What really impacted me, though, was the last event. We built a wall. During this session, individuals would go into a room with Styrofoam blocks and begin to build a wall. Each brick would represent a lie that Satan had told you and you had believed. Once you completed the structure, you would knock down the wall in any fashion you felt led by the Holy Spirit.

I was a little dubious about this at first; I had no idea how this was going to go. I went into the room when it was my turn and I proceeded to build my wall. I used every brick. Satan has been very busy in my mind. Once I had my wall built, I was at a loss as to what to do next. I sat down opposite it and contemplated what I had built.

That's when I noticed that on the bottom row, in the middle, a brick was askew. I walked over to that brick and pulled it out. Every brick toppled. That's when it hit me. They were all lies. There was no substance to it at all. As a matter of fact, with a little bit of truth, the whole thing came crashing down like a house of cards.

A year later, I took some friends to the "Jesus Encounter" and at the time was wondering why I was there. However, I found it to be even more impactful the second time around. I was able to dig in even deeper, working on what had not yet been addressed. What had me wondering, though, was that wall-building room. Would it be as impactful as the last time?

It was my turn. I went in and, as I sat amidst the bricks, I suddenly got a terrible headache. Every time I bent down to pick up a brick the pressure got worse. I couldn't even think straight.

As I sat there in the middle of all the bricks, I felt the Lord say to me, "What are you doing? You already know all the lies; you already built a wall. The question is: What are you going to do about it? Will you continue to let them condemn you and believe the lies? Or will you turn and go in another direction and quit letting them rule over you?"

I looked down at the bricks and decided to build a road instead. After it was built, I walked over it. Now I am working my way through these lies and dismantling the power they have had in my life. Satan loves it when we believe him instead of God. Gods kingdom is an upside-down kingdom. If you try to reason within yourself what God has asked you to do, your reason will talk you out of it. God takes the impossible and makes it possible. Like Peter walking on water. Once out of the boat, there was a storm, and it made him take his eyes off Jesus, and he started to sink. When he got back in the boat, the wind and the waves died down, hmmm. If you're in a storm, take heart, you may just be where you are supposed to be.

PRAYER LANGUAGE

Kat had talked about getting her prayer language at church. I really wasn't sure what she meant. I was not raised Pentecostal, so I was only familiar with the idea of speaking in tongues. To be honest, that thought made me very uncomfortable. But the more she talked about it and the more I read about it, the more I wanted it for myself. I wanted to be able to pray without an agenda. I wanted the Holy Spirit to pray His desire for me, His perfect will. I prayed and prayed and nothing. Nothing worked. My husband and I listened to Robert Morris's series on the Holy Spirit. Morris prayed with those of us watching to receive the Holy Spirit, but we still didn't receive our prayer language—something that is often associated with being baptized in the Holy Spirit.

Then one day while I was in the kitchen, I felt the Lord impress upon me to go for a walk. I grabbed my dog, put him on the leash, and out the door we went. I started praying like I normally do when I walk, but then I felt compelled to make some random noises. Next thing I knew, my prayer took off and I was praying in my prayer language—though to me it sounded like a gibberish. It was crazy.

Later, as I pondered my language, something seemed vaguely familiar about it to me, and I asked the Lord what it was. He gave me a picture of me as a very small girl sitting on the toilet. As I looked down, I could see my feet dangling. I was too small to touch the floor. When I looked up, I could see out the window across the street to the neighbors' house. I used to pretend there was a water slide between their house and mine. I would jump in the tub and slide across the street. At that moment I remembered I had my own language I would "jibber jabber" when I was playing alone. As I thought about it, a light went off in my head. My prayer language was the same language I had been jabbering as a child. I had been praying like this from the very beginning!

Of course, Satan isn't about to let me enjoy a respite from his attacks. Recently he has been trying to make me insecure about my prayer language. I have become aware that, as I have listened to other people's, some sound similar to each other. I found myself comparing and worrying that maybe I didn't have a prayer language after all.

This started to haunt my thoughts. I asked the Lord if I really did receive a language. The next weekend, while I was singing during worship, I opened my mouth to sing praises and my prayer language tumbled out. I have never experienced anything like that before. I was surprised, but my surprise changed to awe and wonder. Like a snap, God laid my fears to rest. If we ask, He is always willing to meet us where we are, but so many times we don't ask.

Later, when I was walking and praying in my prayer language, I thought, "Lord, is this for real? Do you really know what I'm saying? Are You truly interceding and interpreting what is coming out of my mouth?" Immediately, I saw myself from behind. Walking right next to me was Jesus—His head down and cocked towards me and his hand on my shoulder. He was listening!

OUR SECOND YEAR OF IMPACT

During our second year of Impact I started asking questions like, "Lord what can we do as Christians? What can I/we claim as a follower of Jesus Christ?" I continually pondered these questions. One morning, not long after that, while walking with my daughter, she asked if I wanted to help her memorize a verse for a discipleship program, she was doing at our church called Forge and Foundry. That was a first, Kat is good at memorizing, so I was surprised she would ask. Of course, I agreed. Here is the verse she asked for help with:

> I tell you the truth, anyone who believes in me will do the same works I have done, and even greater works, because I am going to be with the Father. You can ask for anything in my name, and I will do it, so that the Son can bring glory to the Father. Yes, ask me for anything in my name, and I will do it! (John 14:12-14, NLT)

What? I had been praying about this very thing. The next morning, I was shocked when I pulled up "the verse of the day" on my Bible app:

> Therefore I tell you, whatever you ask for in prayer, believe that you have received it, and it will be yours. And when you stand praying, if you hold anything against anyone, forgive them, so that your Father in heaven may forgive you your sins. (Mark 11:24-25 NIV)

I started reading the cross-referencing section in my Bible to find all the verses that pertained to this particular one, to see if I could glean any more information on what we can claim. Matthew 17:20 shocked me. I didn't remember this to be a passage that spoke of the things we can claim as Christians.

This verse was part of an account in which the disciples were not able to cast a demon out of a child. Jesus said it was because of their little faith. "Little faith" was underlined, and when I looked it up in the Greek dictionary the word "incredulous" was listed in the definition. I thought that was weird. I looked up the word in Webster's Dictionary, an edition that dates back to 1828. I discovered that the word means "unwilling or unable to believe something."

"What!?" I thought to myself. If I'm unable to fully live out the Christian life because I'm unwilling or unable to ask, speak or believe it, then that's my fault. Jesus says that we will do what He did. In that moment, I realized the reason I might not be seeing or participating in miracles, signs and wonders is because I'm unwilling to step out in faith. It's important to remember that God is sovereign, and His will is what prevails. He might choose not to heal or perform a work, but I will be faithful to at least ask.

The Lord started to show up in random ways during my time in Impact. One day I was walking with Kat, and we were talking about the different directions her life had taken. I told her how I watched her start in one direction and how she ended up in a different one. As we were speaking, the Lord reminded me of a verse in Proverbs 16:9, "We can make our plans, but the Lord determines our steps" (NLT).

As I looked down in that moment, I saw Kat ready to take a step, only there was no ground beneath her foot. The earth had given way and under her foot was an abyss. As I was reaching out to keep her from falling, a step rose up out of nowhere to meet her foot. I thought, "Wow!" That's how it works: we plan what we are going to do, then as we take steps to head in that direction the Lord meets our feet and directs our path. We just need to take a step. If we aren't moving and lifting up our feet, there can be no step. Once we start moving, however, God is able to direct our paths. When we cooperate with him, even if we are headed in a wrong direction, he is able to get us to where He wants us.

In everything I do, my greatest desire is to glorify Jesus. As we were worshipping at Impact one night, I felt the Lord say to me, "When you get to heaven you will get your crowns and lay them at my feet, but do you know how you do that here on earth?" "How Lord?" I asked. He responded: "By giving Me the glory, by glorifying Me here on earth and not taking credit for what I have done." I believe that it is part of the human condition to be prone to the flattery of men, taking credit for what is not ours to take.

One of the subjects we learn about in Impact is prophetic words. Prophetic words are always encouraging. Paul talks about this in 1st Corinthians 14:1 and 3: "Pursue love, and earnestly desire the spiritual gifts, especially that you may prophesy...On the other hand, the one who prophesies speaks to people for their upbuilding, encouragement and consolation" (ESV).

In Impact, we work a lot on hearing God for others. During one of our classes, we were asked to pray and ask God to give us a picture for the person sitting on our right. I got a picture of an old-fashioned truck that was partially restored and partially rusty. I thought, "Really? Is this you Lord or is it me?" I told the person sitting next to me whose son was in rehab that I felt he was partially renewed but still had work to do. The next day as I was walking with my daughter, I was telling her my struggle with the previous night – was that me or was that the Lord? At that same time, I heard a strange rumbling behind us. I turned to look back and there, coming up behind us, was the truck I had seen the night before. "Oh my gosh!" As I pondered the

Holy Spirit's confirmation, what struck me as amazing was to think about what God had to do to get that truck there just as I was asking that question! There is a verse in Isaiah 65 that says that He is at work answering our prayers before we even know to ask. God is not put off or bothered by our questions, ask Him for clarity.

DREAMS

I firmly believe that God gives us dreams. I don't believe that all of our dreams are from God, but I believe He uses dreams just as much now as He always has. With that being said, I'm not much of a dreamer. I have asked for dreams and desired them, but for the most part I've had to be happy with the occasional one here and there.

There are, however, four dreams that have changed and rocked my world. They have been so impactful that they have changed the course of my actions.

Dream 1: I dreamt our family was in Yellowstone staying in a condo of some sort. We were being chased by a grizzly bear that was missing half of an arm, and he was furious. He started chasing us and was gaining on us. We ran into the condo and slammed the door. He blew through that door, so we ran into the bedroom and barricaded ourselves inside. He could not get in.

He quieted down and we sat in that room for hours, until Eric thought he was gone. I did not want to go out, but Eric insisted, so we went into the kitchen and it was quiet. Amelia was a baby, so I put her in her highchair. Just then that crazy bear came around the corner from the dining room, and we all ran out. I suddenly remembered that Amelia was still in her highchair. I turned around to see the bear standing over her shaking his head and bellowing. Spit was flying everywhere. I cried out, "Oh God!" Immediately the bear flew across the room, turned into a little stuffed teddy bear and dropped to the floor.

The dream ended just like those old Looney-Tune cartoons always did when a circle would close to black and Bugs Bunny would say, "That's all folks." Instead, I heard a voice say, "that's what happens for those who call upon the name of The Lord."

You see, I was dealing with a lot of fear and anxiety at that point. Even though our kids were all out of the house, I was getting hit with fear for their safety, and for mine and Eric's. The Lord gave me this dream, and it gave me peace.

Dream 2: I was struggling in my relationship with the Lord and I could not figure out why. In this dream I was dating a guy. I really didn't like him and was trying to figure out how to break up with him. Then out of nowhere there came a girl who was very interested in him. You would think I would be happy, but instead I was so jealous and tried everything I could to get him back. Then I woke up.

As I was recounting this dream to one of my kids, I felt the Lord saying to me, "There are times when you are ambivalent towards me, but once you see someone in a close relationship with me, that's when you are interested in me again. You have to choose and stay the course. Ouch! He was right. God seeks relationship. He is not satisfied with anything less. I had to decide whether I was all in or not.

Dream 3: More changes in my life prompted me to ask the Lord one night, "What about me? Do you have something more for me?" I dreamt that my daughters, Kat and Amelia, were on a bus going to the shopping mall with me. When we got there, the mall was just one long hallway. There were restaurants and shops on both sides of the hall, and one was a new restaurant that looked interesting.

In a matter of minutes, Amelia was missing. I kept asking Kat where she went, but she wouldn't tell me. The next thing I knew, Kat was missing too. We were supposed to get ourselves lunch for the ride back. When I got back on the bus, Kat and Amelia had their lunches from these great restaurants, but because I had spent all my time looking for them, my lunch was a bag of McDonald's. I was so upset because my time had been wasted looking for them, and they did not seem in the least bit concerned.

When I woke up, I was so mad at them. At first, I didn't think this was a "God dream", but as I recounted it to Amelia, I could see the dots start to line up. I realized that I am so concerned with what my kids are doing and being a part of their lives, that I'm not doing the things God has for me to do. So, instead of having a great lunch of my own, I ended up with McDonald's. Are you missing the good thing He has for you because you are preoccupied with what He is doing for someone else?

Dream 4: I dreamt that my brother was getting married,

and I was supposed to help decorate for the wedding. I was being lazy and didn't really want to. When other tasks presented themselves outside of the wedding, I was happy to do them. I missed helping my brother on his big day and, while I was getting ready to go to the wedding, he died. I never saw him again. I woke up with such sorrow. That's when I realized I was supposed to write this book; if I didn't, I knew I would feel that same regret.

I had another dream that same night. I was in a car and in the back seat there was a partial denture rolling around. When I woke up, I thought, "Oh, that's Rob's tooth!" My brother, Rob, had worn a partial denture since he was a boy. The fact I dreamed about it shocked me. I then remembered hearing Pastor Shawn Bolz talk about an encounter he had with a family during a prophetic night. He received a vision of a little boy—who they later identified as the family's nephew—who had died and was in heaven praying for his own brother. When I reflected on my dream, I was immediately reminded of Bolz's testimony: "Rob is praying for me." My daughter Kat—who had listened to the same message—said the same thing as soon as I told her.

GOD'S PROTECTION

Sometimes I do things without thinking them through, and God graciously has protected me. My friend Ellen and I took a cruise to Mexico, Honduras and Belize. I had heard that Roatan has the second-largest barrier reef in the world, and I felt that I should go scuba-diving as long as I was there. I hadn't been scuba-diving in years, and I had only been once before that, but I was determined.

I made my reservation and, with some amount of trepidation on my part, I went down to meet the dive group. I started to feel a little more nervous when I saw my fellow divers. Two guys looked like Navy Seals. Another passenger was a dive instructor, and everyone had their own wet suits and weights. I couldn't even remember how my Buoyancy Compensator Device (BCD) jacket worked. On the inside I was trying to figure out how to get out of the dive, though I acted like I knew what I was doing.

The day consisted of two dives in two locations. The first dive went well. It took a while to get acclimated to everything and for the awkwardness to subside, but once it did, my confidence grew.

During the second dive, I was not so lucky. I had too much weight in my jacket and I could not get off the ocean floor. Our dive master didn't want us adding air to our BCD jackets for whatever reason, but I was starting to panic. I was dragging along the ocean floor, and I began to hyperventilate.

Finally, out of desperation I hid behind some coral and added air to my jacket. That was much better. The panic was gone but I still couldn't get my breathing under control. I kept looking at our boat, trying to figure out how long it would take to ascend to prevent me from getting decompression sickness.

Right at that moment—when my anxiety was maxed out and I was using up all kinds of oxygen—a green moray eel came out of nowhere. It swam up to me and ran right into my forehead before backing up and staring at my face. It ran into my forehead again, and then proceeded to swim around me. I was mesmerized. I couldn't take my eyes off it. It kept swimming around me before taking off suddenly. After it left, I realized I was breathing normally and was able to finish the dive. I really felt the Lord intervened for me that day. Why? Because nothing is by chance.

LESSONS:

Once I realized how much God actually wanted to speak to me it transformed how I started to listen. I started realizing that, while reading my Bible, I wasn't reading to hear so much as getting through my daily reading plan. Even though reading through the Bible in a year is good, it was too much for me to really hear what God was saying. So, I stopped to reevaluate. I discovered that my reading plan was too much to really *hear* any one specific word or idea. To combat this, I started to read one chapter at a time—slowly—paying close attention to the actual words being used and how they were put together. Then I would sit and ponder what I read, rolling it over and over in my mind. I also realized I read the Word so familiarly that I was not concentrating on what was being said, I was just skimming it. I decided to read the Bible in a different translation, for me that was The Message. Reading this version, a paraphrase of the Bible, changed everything—it was completely different from any other translations. The Word began to pop and was actually moving from my head to my heart! What follows in this chapter are just a few of the ways that God started to speak to me through His Word as I actively started *listening* instead of just reading.

One lesson I learned came from John 4. Jesus didn't come just so that we could be with Him in heaven. No, He came to restore a right relationship with God—a relationship that was lost in the Garden of Eden when sin entered—so that we don't have to live this life alone. He came to bring peace in every circumstance in our lives. There is a woman that is told of in John 4, she is simply called the "woman at the well." I like that because she can represent me, and if you think about it, she could be you too. She was an outcast—how many of us haven't felt that way inside from time to time. She had to go to the well at the hottest time of the day. This particular day started like every other, except that today she had a divine appointment. Jesus was at the well, and he asked her for a drink of water. She thought it odd that a Jewish man would ask her, a Samaritan, for a drink. She responds to him, "How is it that you a Jew would ask me a Samaritan for a drink?" Jesus answered, "If you knew who it was you were talking to you would have asked me to give you living water and I would give it to you." He then said to her, "Go call your husband." She replied: "I have no husband." Jesus already knew this: "You have spoken correctly, in fact, you have had five husbands and the one you are now with is not your husband."

Did you know that in those days a woman wasn't allowed to divorce her husband, only a man could divorce his spouse? So here she is, five times rejected, and even now the guy she is with won't marry her. As I read this account it suddenly occurred to me that she had an empty hole in her that she was trying to fill with men/relationships. I thought to myself: "How many times have I tried to fill that hole with relationships, shopping/clothes, food, really anything other than God?" None of those things ever worked, they only left me needing more.

Jesus continues in his conversation with the woman: "If you knew who was talking to you *you* would have *asked*, and I would give you living water." I realized then that I have to ask Jesus to fill me. It's a relationship, not a "one and done." He wants us to talk to Him, to listen to Him. When I put my faith and trust in Him, He sent His Holy Spirit to live in me. The Holy Spirit will never leave me. He isn't called the Counselor and Comforter for nothing. Does that mean that life becomes a bowl of cherries? No, but it means that I never have to do life alone again. I have found that I am turning to Jesus sooner than ever before, when I'm feeling hemmed in, angry or insecure. I stop and tell God my need—that I can't change these feelings—and ask Him to help. He never fails to bring me into a spacious place of peace. But it takes me confessing my need, like He told the woman at the well. "If you would *ask* me, I would give you living water." My problem is I don't always feel like asking. Sometimes I'm obstinate and just want to sit in my junk, but when I do ask, then comes peace. As I pondered "the woman at the well" I realized that Jesus wasn't talking to her just about eternal life, but living water, real life here and now, regardless of circumstances. He was offering her freedom and relationship. He offers that same thing to you and me, but like her, we have to receive it.

Throughout my childhood I've experienced my share of rejection. Because of that rejection, I learned early on that the only one who I could depend on was me. I would deflect with humor to protect myself from hurt. This made me very self-focused. When you have done this for years, the love that 1st Corinthians 13 talks about is something that was not easy for me to grasp. Then, one day as I was reading it again, taking my time and changing translations, the Holy Spirit started to minister to me. I realized, "I CAN'T DO THIS! I, in myself, do not have the ability to love this way." I sincerely tried, but inevitably I would always get in the way.

Paul's words became an indictment against me. I would read that if I can speak in tongues of angels, fathom all mysteries, have all knowledge, and have the faith to move mountains—but if I don't have love, then all these gifts mean nothing (1st Cor. 13: 1-2, NIV). I would feel condemnation and say to myself, "I am a gong, because I don't know how to do this." That's where I was when the Holy Spirit took over.

My first mistake was my interjection of that little word "do". "Do" leaves me with the thought it's something I attain in my own strength. We love the word "do"; we love the rules and traditions that go with it. The word "do" makes us feel like we did something to deserve certain treatment. Jesus came to get rid of all those rules we can't keep. But freedom can be a tough pill to swallow, Jesus fulfilled the law, because we couldn't. So, what do we do? We add our own meaningless rules and traditions that we still can't keep, to feel like we are *right* with God. Rules like "no dancing," "no movies" and "no cards," because they may lead us into sin. So here I was, trying to be patient, trying to be kind, and forgiving according to my own standard. The result? I was an epic fail.

So, what do I do now? The right answer is "nothing." He does it all. I must learn to lean into Him, to believe that He is going to do what he says He will. My job is to be like John when he would recline against Jesus: Talking, listening and being quiet. I kept trying to make it about me. What I didn't get was that it's not about me at all. It's about Jesus. If I do all these things out of selfish ambition, I am no longer showing you the face of Christ but rather my own. I have to let God work through me. I have to learn to love from Him out, doing those things He lays on my heart. I have to trust that if it's important enough for Him to say it, then He is going to do it. It hit me like a ton of bricks, "God can't lie!" If He says He is the one who changes us, He means it, otherwise He couldn't have said it.

God's love is not based on emotion. It's a choice. Simply put, my emotions run amuck, I'm up one day and down the next. I might get upset because I read a text wrong, or for some reason I feel rejected. My emotions, my feelings are not trustworthy. I love the way Hannah Whitehall Smith sums up feelings in her book, *The Christian's Secret of a Happy Life*: "Feelings are like clamoring, crying children in a nursery. My will is the mother. I am not to be held captive by my children's whims and desires, but to bend their will to mine for both our sakes" (1952, p. 86).

This is where I'm at now. I'm still in the Word every day but I take smaller bites. I'm a lot quieter, giving Him a chance to speak. I am learning to be present with the Lord all day by having a running conversation with Him. He directs me with ideas that I can do for others and brings divine conversations. Rather than catering to my feelings, I am learning to *choose* love. I don't always do it perfectly, but Jesus did. His grace covers my lack. If I'm made aware of a need, I try to meet it. There is a lot more joy when I operate out of His desires rather then saying yes to every person who asks, because I'm afraid to say no.

Have you ever noticed that some mornings you just don't feel like reading your Bible? This is where I was one rainy morning when out of obedience, I started reading my daily chapter. On this particular day, the Holy Spirit opened my eyes to something I had read a hundred times and never thought much about:

> Zechariah and Elizabeth were righteous in God's eyes, careful to obey all of the Lord's commandments and regulations. They had no children because Elizabeth

> was unable to conceive, and they were both very old. One day Zechariah was serving God in the Temple, for his order was on duty that week. As was the custom of the priests, he was chosen by lot to enter the sanctuary of the Lord and burn incense. While the incense was being burned, a great crowd stood outside praying. While Zechariah was in the sanctuary, an angel of the Lord appeared to him, standing to the right of the incense altar. Zechariah was shaken and overwhelmed with fear when he saw him. But the angel said, "Don't be afraid, Zechariah! God has heard your prayer. Your wife, Elizabeth, will give you a son and you are to name him John…" (Luke 1: 6-13, NLT)

As I was reading this passage, I was struck that it says, "Zechariah and Elizabeth were very old." Even though they were old in age, the angel goes on to say God has heard their prayer and they were going to have a son. It's no wonder that Zechariah was perplexed. He probably didn't remember the last time he had prayed for a child. Now the angel shows up and says, "your prayer has been heard," as if they were being prayed in real time. After reading this, it hit me, God stands outside of time, He is not limited by time like we are. He created it! "Wow, I bet my prayers are always before God. Prayers that I prayed a long time ago, and prayers I prayed just today, and prayers I've forgotten about. It's all in God's timing."

How quick I am to be angry when my prayers are not answered on my timetable. I never stop to ask myself, "what am I doing right now? What important work does God have me doing that I think is mundane? Is it washing the dishes? Am I being faithful in the little things He asks me to do?" Jesus said that if I'm not faithful in the small things, how can He trust me for those that are bigger?

That being said, maybe it's just timing. Is the time right? Zachariah and Elizabeth waited a really long time for the time to be right, until they were *old*. The question is, are we ready? We pray Ephesians 3:20 all the time: "Now to Him who is able to do immeasurably more than all I can ask or imagine…" (NIV). But God doesn't set us up for failure, He uses everything to build us so that we are ready for the immeasurably more than we can ask or imagine. We get prophetic words spoken over us and our expectation is that it's just around the corner. Not necessarily. Sometimes it takes years, decades, to get us ready. How do we get ready? We keep moving forward, we do not sit idly and wait. We may need schooling, maturing, or maybe just a few lessons in humility.

After reading this passage, I received a picture of God sitting on His throne from behind and all these prayers before Him, fluttering in the air. Prayers from my beginning until now—ones long forgotten by me—but not forgotten by Him. He reminded me how as a small child I used to pray to have a real family life. Times that we would have picnics in the park and play games and just be a family, sadly they never happened. When my mother married my stepdad, I was 13 and I stopped praying those prayers. However, what I prayed for as a child, were still before Him. Even though I had forgotten all about it, God did not. God showed me how He answered that prayer as an adult with my own family. Once I had my own kids, I basically got a do over from my childhood. The answer to that prayer was no less sweet many years later as an adult. Had He not reminded me; I would have missed it. Have you lost heart due to the passage of time? Do you feel like your dreams have fallen to the ground? Take courage from Zachariah and Elizabeth, nothing is too hard or too late for God.

A reoccurring fear for me has been the fear of death. My fear stemmed mostly from not wanting my kids to grow up without a mother or someone else being their mother. Heck, in all honesty, I don't want to be left out or forgotten. Therefore, it was no surprise to me, as I was reading through the Gospels, the Holy Spirit decided it was time to deal with this fear of death. I came to a passage in John 8:51 and 11:25-26 that stopped me in my tracks. The first passage reads, "Very truly I tell you, whoever obeys my word will never see death" (NIV). The second is as follows: "Jesus said to her, I am the resurrection and the life. The one who believes in me will live, even though they die. And whoever lives by believing in me will never die" (NIV).

It finally occurred to me that I can only truly live when I'm no longer afraid of death, and not until then. You see, if we're always worried about our lives, we protect ourselves and play it safe. However, when we put our faith and trust in Jesus, we know the outcome and can truly live for Him without fear of death. Hebrews 2:14-15 says this:

> Since the children have flesh and blood, He too shared in their humanity so that by His death he might break the power of him who holds the power of death—that is, the devil—and free those who all their lives were held in slavery by their fear of death. (NIV)

In this passage, we see that Jesus holds the keys of eternal life. He made this known so humankind would not have to worry and could live life to the fullest. He knew that if we are always worried about our lives we will always be trying to protect and preserve them.

God gives us chances to join Him in battle. The problem is usually the odds. Israel's story is one of the odds always being stacked against them. God invites us to the battle. Do we join, do we trust Him? Staying home is safe and no one gets hurt but joining Him means life and death struggles—a lot of times it means death to myself. It can mean flying by the seat of your pants—for me, the life I've always dreamed of. Here is my question, will I let fear stop me from the wild ride of seeing God do "above and beyond of all I can ask or imagine" (Ephesians 3:20, NIV)? My prayer is this: "Lord give me direction, give me a door to walk through. I want to be a willing participant, even if I'm white knuckling it and my stomach hurts."

How often do you memorize verses and instead of actually doing what the verse says you spit it out over and over again and can't figure out why you are still stuck and have no peace. I am notorious for this. I have memorized verses, without putting them into practice except to spit them back out again. I have never really camped on them and let them change me. This hit me recently as I was rememorizing Philippians 4:8. "Finally brothers, whatever is true, whatever is noble, whatever is right, whatever is pure, whatever is lovely, whatever is admirable -- if anything is excellent or praiseworthy think about such things" (NIV).

I realized that God is not asking me to simply spit out this verse, but to get my mind wrapped around it. He wants me to think about what *is* true, noble, and righteous. Do you see the difference? We need to do what it is saying rather than just repeating the verse over and over. We need to *think* on "these things" and focus on what they are. If you're not having victory in your life, think about what you're thinking about. Don't think it's necessarily a salvation issue—particularly if you have already put your faith in Jesus. It might be a thought problem—think about what you are actually thinking about.

I love the fact that even when we go on vacation, and take a break from our normal schedules, God doesn't take breaks. He is always ready to use every opportunity to teach a lesson.

While Caleb and I were in Africa, the Holy Spirit impressed upon me 2nd Kings 17:34: "They (Israel) worshiped the Lord, but also served their own gods in accordance with the customs of the nations from which they had been brought" (NIV). This verse hit home for me after I returned home from Kenya. What I saw while there was a way of life that was far simpler and less encumbered by material possessions. The men and women I met, though having less in material wealth, had far more peace and joy than I. Never before have I seen how worthless the things are in which I put my time, money and energy. I have been bogged down serving my own gods daily, gods of my own making, and because of this I have been prone to falling away.

We go to church on Sunday and we worship God with our lips. We sing praises to Him with our hands held high. We say and do what is good and acceptable at church and we feel it with all our hearts. But when we go home, we serve gods of our own making: whether our families, cars, homes, clothes, power, money, body image, sports, time, or travel. None of these things in and of themselves are bad or wrong, only when they become our focus. If there is anything in your life that you say you can't live without, and it's not Jesus, it's time to re-evaluate.

God then impressed upon me that, though we may not practice child sacrifice literally, we do it all the same. When our kids see us bow down to the idols of today (i.e. sports, wealth, power, appearance, etc.), they will do as we do. It will be all they have ever known, a stumbling block for them. Our gods, our idols and our battles will become theirs. We literally sacrifice our kids into the fire of our desires, our dreams and our wants.

As I was remembering and writing these lessons down, a thought occurred to me: "Is it any wonder why Jesus keeps telling me to give my kids to Him?" My kids are that "thing" I feel I couldn't live without if something were to happen to them. They are one of my gods. I must remember God is the answer to all my needs. Everything, and I do mean everything, flows through His final act of sacrifice. Our salvation comes only through Him. He is the one who never did anything wrong, who stayed on the cross and then gave up His life for us. He deserves to be the only God in my life.

I challenge you Dear Reader, to take some time and ask the Lord to show you what idols you have in your life, and then, dethrone them.

BITS AND PIECES

God is faithful. We don't think about that every day but when it does come up, we are so grateful. Our son, Caleb, had gone on a week-long mountain-biking trip with his friends. They rode hard for most of the trip. We had been worried because he was going to be home for only 12 hours before having to turn around and get up the next morning at 4 a.m. to drive from Missoula to Estes Park, Colorado.

As soon as I heard his plans, warning bells started going off in my head, and I started praying for his safety. That night I went to bed and forgot all about it, but at about 3 a.m. I woke up and couldn't fall back to sleep. To be honest, I still did not think about Caleb's trip.

Still the feeling to pray persisted. I was bothered but didn't know why. I decided to go through the ABC's of God's attributes and then the ABC's of things I was thankful for. This went on until about 4:30 a.m.

I finally fell asleep only to be woken up about 15 minutes later by the phone ringing. It was Caleb: "Mom, I'm okay." What? That's when I remembered he was going to be driving. Caleb had hit an elk on the interstate and demolished his car. To see the pictures, you would have never believed he and his co-worker walked away without a scratch. The elk didn't. I praise God for His faithfulness even when I forget.

Once while worshipping in Impact I had a picture of a dirt path with many boulders lying in it. As we continued to worship, the boulders started flying out of the way. I felt the Lord was saying that, as we seek Him and worship Him, the boulders that seem to be in our way are going to get out of our way. If you feel like your prayers are not being heard and God seems far from you, start praising Him, spend time worshiping Him and just be quiet before Him. It won't take long and you will feel his nearness once again.

Sometimes as I'm going about my day, not really thinking about anything, the Lord takes it upon Himself to speak to my heart. On this day, as I was lifting weights, I started thinking about how sweet my husband is to so many people. I felt the Lord impress something on me as I reflected on my husband's character: "Rebecca, you always look to the 'popular people,' but they aren't the ones who need you. They will always have somebody just by virtue of their popularity. You need to be looking for those who are alone. You need to help those who are new or feel awkward to feel more at home and at ease. They are your priority, and He is right. Let's be people who look for the one.

Here is a demonstration of just the sweet goodness of God. Eric and I went to the Oregon coast to get away. While we were there, we spent some time in a little town called Oceanside. While eating at the Blue Agate Café, we noticed their collection of agates which the owners had found on the beach just across the street. Intrigued, we set off for the shore after breakfast to search. Although it was high tide, we were able to go through the tunnel and get to a rocky beach where we started to look.

As we made our way down the beach, we couldn't find any agates and Eric needed to go back to the hotel. I decided to wait for him on the beach and keep looking for the elusive agate. As I was waiting for Eric, the ocean was so loud that I decided to take that time to praise God and shout my love for Him. It was just Him, me and the surf.

As I stood on a rock looking at the sand and sea swirling around my feet, I rededicated my life to the Lord. Below me there was nothing but sand, a completely smooth area. As I watched, the tide came in and the water bubbled at my feet. The tide went out again and I looked up at the sky and laughed. When I looked down, there in the sand all by itself, was a beautiful and clear agate. It was huge! It was placed so sweetly at the base of the rock I was standing on—such a treasure.

Just then, Eric returned and a woman walked up to him with two friends looking at what he had collected along the shore. They were telling him all about his rocks and shells. I walked up and showed the woman my agate. She was amazed. She said to me, "you might as well stop looking now because you have found 'the best.'" She asked where I had found it and I told her that I had been standing on the rock praying and when the wave went out, there it was.

She asked if I had been sick, and I said, "No, I was just rededicating my life back to the Lord…*again*." She looked at me, reached out and grabbed my face, bringing it close to hers. She then wrapped me in a huge hug before going on her way. Lord, was she one of your angels? She was tattered and worn but oh so sweet. A year later, the Lord reminded me of that time while I was listening to a song called "What Do I Know of Holy" by Addison Road. As I was singing the Lord reminded me of the woman I thought was an angel. He said "that wasn't an angel, it was Me." As soon as He said that, a line of the song came on that sang, "if You touched my face would I know You, looked into my eyes could I behold you?" I was wrecked. I believe God loves to be part of every aspect of our lives, and to show he knows our hearts and how to speak to us in a way that we know its Him.

I love it when the Lord speaks to me and I question, question, question Him, and then He eventually gets around to knocking it out of the park. On our way to an Impact retreat one weekend, I was reading a book called *One Word That Will Change Your Life* by Jon Gordon, Dan Britton and Jimmy Page. The premise is that, instead of making a bunch of new year's resolutions you can't keep, you should pray and ask the Lord to give you one word to focus on for the entire year. That sounded great to me, so I went through the directions and prayed for a word. I kept thinking of all the words that would be "good" words to get—words like "intentional", "love" and "seek", but I wasn't getting anything from God.

I read the book out loud to Eric, and I was irritated when I realized he wasn't paying attention. When we pulled into the retreat venue, I shut the book with a flourish. As soon as it snapped shut, I heard "obedience!" What?! That was not among the words I was considering. Nevertheless, obedience became my word for the year.

About five months later, at another Impact retreat, our leader Beth asked us to pray and ask the Lord for a word for the upcoming Impact year. Asking for a word always makes me nervous. I don't question His ability to speak, just my ability to hear. She told us to pray, so I closed my eyes and right away heard, "Listen." I was confused: "Listen? Listen to what? Is that the word?"

I never heard any other words, so I assumed "listen" was it. Other people had words like "victorious" and "illuminate" which made me feel like I had gotten a rock (like Charlie Brown). When I got home, I decided to look up every verse that had the word "listen" in it. There were only eight, and the first one was in Exodus. I looked up the Hebrew meaning of the word and was shocked. One meaning for listen was "obedience." The Hebrew dictionary continued with this interesting observation: "Historically, the Jewish people never listened without planning to obey" (Hebrew Greek Key Word Study Bible, ESV)). Not only was this a good lesson for me, but a life lesson as well.

IN HIS PRESENCE

I hate nighttime because I struggle sleeping through the night. I recall a specific night when I was unable to sleep. At 3 a.m. I was up, and I moved into the office to pray. I had a hard time focusing, so I decided to pray in my prayer language. As I sat there speaking, I had the distinct feeling that I was sitting on my daddy's lap just babbling away. I could feel the pleasure and delight of the Lord; He listened to me like He had nothing better to do and was in no hurry to leave. Neither was I. I stayed there for hours, yet it only seemed like a few moments. Dear Reader, God wants to spend time with you just like that. Linger with Him, you won't regret it.

During these nights awake, I sometimes go through the ABC's of God's attributes. For every letter, I come up with three or four attributes that start with that letter, and I praise Him with them. In recent years, I have been so afraid of losing my mind that I didn't even want to talk much out of fear of forgetting words. On this particular night, I remember coming to V and saying, "Vanquish. You vanquish all my enemies." I must have fallen asleep right at that point.

In the morning I had such a sweet time of reading His Word, but still my underlying fear had its usual grip, dampening my joy in His presence. When I got in my car later that morning, I remembered the previous evening I had been listening to "Your Love Is Strong" by Cory Asbury. I must have been midway through it when I turned off the car because, when I turned the car on the artist was singing, "Your love vanquished all my enemies. It broke the chains that silenced me and set this songbird free." Something leapt within my spirit. I knew the Lord was talking to me. It wasn't like, "Bam!", and no more trouble with word finding. It was more like the story of the 10 lepers in Luke 17: 11-19. As I go, I am healing and I haven't struggled near as much since. I just kind of noticed it was gone. Satan, however, would love to convince me otherwise, try to get me to "reason" within myself and rob me of a victory, But, the Bible says stand firm, so I am.

PARTING THOUGHTS

God speaks. He speaks a lot more often than we might think. In telling you my story my hope is that you look back at your own life and those times you thought were just a "coincidence" were really and truly you hearing God. But hearing is not enough.

If I treat the lessons that the Lord has given me as experiences only, if I have not allowed them to change me, then why should I receive them in the first place? If I spit out these encounters for other people to learn from but don't heed them myself, or if—God forbid—my faith remains the same, then I will have missed the whole point.

When God speaks into areas of our lives, He gives us opportunities to grow. Today as I was reading in Proverbs, I came across a verse that stopped me in my tracks: "If you punish a mocker, the simpleminded will learn a lesson; if you correct the wise, they will be all the wiser" (Proverbs 19: 25, NLT).

Whether I'm being reprimanded or exhorted, I don't want God to speak to me and just learn a lesson, without applying it to my life. I want God to speak to me and become someone who is wiser, and whose faith is stronger, because I continually reflect and heed it.

May our dear Father in heaven richly bless you, and may you become ever increasingly aware of the ways He has spoken and will continue to speak into your life. God is not hiding from you. He wants you to hear Him, and He has so much to say.

ABOUT THE AUTHOR

"My mother was very influential in my coming to faith in Christ. When the Lord started drawing me closer to Him through His word, it was in large part my mother to whom I went with scriptural questions. The Lord used her to patiently encourage in me an open mind."

~ Caleb Schwartzkopf

***

"I consider myself immeasurably blessed to have grown up with a woman who was so open and honest about her faith. My mother lives out her faith authentically, teaching from her experiences all along the way. She has shown us that Jesus is real, God truly speaks, and He wants you to hear His voice. Now, I, my father and siblings are no longer the only ones who can benefit from her journey."

~ Kat Hussain (Schwartzkopf)

***

"When I think of my mother, I will always remember her as she was in the early morning: sitting-up in bed, coffee in her hand, and reading glasses on, with about a half dozen books sprawled across her lap. Every morning, I would find her pouring over the Scriptures. That daily act marked me as a child; it showed me that Jesus was meant for more than just Sunday mornings. My mother's relationship with the Lord has and always will inspire my own."

~ Amelia Schwartzkopf

**** If you would like to connect with Rebecca, you can email her at hespeaks.rs@gmail.com ****

Printed in the United States
By Bookmasters